FOR GRACE WILKINSON, ALICE WILKINSON
& EMILY WILKINSON.

THANK YOU TO THE SHEERLUCKIAN PARANORMAL PUZZLE TEAM:
EMILY GRACE BLACKHAM AND OLIVER GEORGE BLACKHAM.

© Copyright 2018

Dean Wilkinson and Joseph Keen

The right of Dean Wilkinson and Joseph Keen to be identified as the author and illustrator of this work has been asserted by them in accordance with the Copyright, Designs and Patents Act 1998.

All rights reserved. No reproduction, copy or transmission of this publication may be made without express prior written permission. No paragraph of this publication may be reproduced, copied or transmitted except with express prior written permission or in accordance with the provisions of the Copyright Act 1956 (as amended). Any person who commits any unauthorised act in relation to this publication may be liable to criminal prosecution
and civil claims for damage.

All characters appearing in this work are fictitious or used fictitiously. Except for certain historical personages, any resemblance
to real persons, living or dead, is purely coincidental.
The opinions expressed herein are those of the author
and not of MX Publishing.

Paperback ISBN 978-1-78705-364-9
ePub ISBN 978-1-78705-365-6
PDF ISBN 978-1-78705-366-3

Published by MX Publishing

335 Princess Park Manor, Royal Drive,
London, N11 3GX
www.mxpublishing.co.uk

Cover by Joseph Keen

Sheerluck
Versus The Paranormal

By Dean Wilkinson & Joseph Keen

CONTENTS

- 7 INTRODUCTION
- 9 CHARLIE CHARLIE
- 19 THE SHEERLUCKIAN ARMOURY – PSYCHOMETER
- 20 MRS HUDSON WHO'S WHO
- 21 THE SHEERLUCKIAN ARMOURY – FARADAY BAG
- 22 THE CLONE ZONE
- 23 THE SHEERLUCKIAN ARMOURY – DIMENSIONAL DOOR KNOB
- 24 MYCROFT'S MINI FILES – GEF THE TALKING MONGOOSE
- 26 TELEPORT BY NUMBERS
- 27 BLACK EYED CHILDREN
- 38 MYCROFT'S MINI FILES – THE VIOGE, A FLESH EATING SCARECROW
- 40 FOW-ST WHO'S WHO
- 41 NOTLAND YARD IDENTITY PARADE
- 42 WHERE'S WHERE – COLISEUM OF THE DAMNED
- 44 MYTHAMATICS
- 45 THE LIE-COCULARS
- 46 WHERE'S WHERE – THE NOT
- 47 WHERE'S WHERE – NOTLAND YARD
- 48 GHOULS
- 60 THE FATAL ADDER DAGGERS
- 62 THE SHEERLUCKIAN ARMOURY – THE I-SCREAM-VAN
- 63 THE I-SCREAM-VAN
- 64 THE YORKSHIRE DRAGOON WHO'S WHO
- 65 UNION FLAG FIND
- 66 MYCROFT'S MINI FILES – THE GREEN CHILDREN OF WOOLPIT
- 68 ASTRAL PROJECTION
- 79 JUDGE MENTAL
- 80 CHRISTMAS MOURNING
- 82 WITCH IZZIT AND IMPOSEALS WHO'S WHO
- 83 WHICH IS IT?
- 84 YOUR VINYL BREATH RECORD SHOP
- 86 HAVE YOU LIVED BEFORE?
- 90 PUZZLE ANSWERS
- 92 OTHER BOOKS FROM THE AUTHOR

INTRODUCTION

'THERE ARE MORE THINGS IN HEAVEN AND EARTH, HORATIO, THAN ARE DREAMT OF IN YOUR PHILOSOPHY.'
FROM HAMLET BY BILL SHAKESPEARE

SHAKEY WAS QUITE CORRECT WHEN HE WROTE THIS. BUT, IF HE'D KNOWN JUST HOW MIND-BOGGLINGLY STRANGE AND TERRIFYING SOME OF THOSE 'THINGS' ARE HE WOULD HAVE WET HIS TIGHTS.

THE AVERAGE PERSON SEES LESS THAN 10% OF THE UNIVERSE. THERE ARE EXTRAORDINARY AND BIZARRE THINGS AT WORK IN THIS WORLD 24/7. BAD THINGS. WICKED THINGS. THERE ARE OTHER DIMENSIONS AND REALMS FILLED WITH WEIRD, CONFUSING AND ALL TOGETHER BLOOD-CURDLING MONSTERS, GRIM GHOSTS, VICIOUS DEVILS, SUPERNATURAL CRIMINALS AND OTHER REALLY BIZARRE STUFF.

THANKFULLY, WE'VE GOT SHEERLUCK, WATSON AND MYCROFT TO PROTECT US.

THE GHOSTBUSTERS MIGHT HAVE SAID 'I AINT AFRAID OF NO GHOST.' (THEY WEREN'T AFRAID OF INCORRECT GRAMMAR EITHER), BUT THESE BRITISH BOGEYMAN BASHERS AREN'T AFRAID OF ANYTHING.

IN THIS SERIES OF BOOKS WE EXAMINE ELEMENTS OF THE PARANORMAL HUMANS HAVE REPORTED OVER THE CENTURIES. WATSON AND MYCROFT INVESTIGATE EACH UNCANNY ANOMALY AND DISSECT IT BEFORE GIVING IT A SHEERLUCKIAN RATING.

SPOOKINESS 07
REAL DANGER 08
A.D.P. LEVEL 04
HOKUM RATING 03

HOW SCARY IS IT?
COULD IT HARM YOU?
HOW MUCH ACTUAL DOCUMENTED PROOF IS THERE?
HOKUM MEANS DRIVEL, BULL DROPPINGS OR LIES AND FIBS.

SHEERLUCK THEN TELLS US A TALE ABOUT HOW HE ENCOUNTERED SOMETHING EERILY SIMILAR AND KICKED ITS PARANORMAL BOTTOM WITH AMAZING OTHERWORLDLY DEDUCTION, WEAPONRY AND, OF COURSE, SHEER LUCK.

CHARLIE CHARLIE

SPOOKINESS 02
REAL DANGER 03
A.D.P. LEVEL 02
HOKUM RATING 06

Fun for all the family!
Age 6-66

YOU MIGHT THINK CHARLIE CHARLIE, OR THE PENCIL GAME, IS A NEW PHENOMENON, BUT YOU'D BE EVEN MORE WRONG THAN LORD WRONGLY WRONG OF WRONGNESS MANOR, WRONGSHIRE, WAS ABOUT PRETTY MUCH EVERYTHING.

IT'S AS OLD AS A REALLY OLD THING. LEGEND HAS IT CHARLIE IS A TERRIBLE MEXICAN DEMON WHO WILL ANSWER YOUR QUESTIONS, YES OR NO, BUT IF THE WHIM TAKES HIM HE WILL SCARE THE LIVING BREAKFAST OUT OF YOU!

INDEED.
HE WILL CURSE AND HAUNT YOU WITH DIRE CONSEQUENCES.
A BIT LIKE MEXICAN FOOD – OH WAIT – THAT'S DIARRHOEA CONSEQUENCES.

GROSS. TO PLAY CHARLIE CHARLIE YOU WRITE DOWN 'YES' AND 'NO' TWICE AND PLACE THE WORDS IN A SQUARE SHAPE.
LAY ONE PENCIL DOWN FLAT THEN BALANCE THE SECOND ONE ON TOP OF IT TO MAKE A CROSS SHAPE.

SPOT ON MYCROFT. THEN, YOU HAVE TO INVITE CHARLIE TO 'PLAY' BEFORE YOU MAY ASK HIM YOUR QUESTION.
SO, FOR EXAMPLE, IF YOU ASK 'AM I GOING TO DIE HORRIBLY?' AND THE POINT OF THE PENCIL MOVES TO A YES – YOU'D BETTER KISS YOUR SANITY GOODBYE.
WE ADVISE ASKING CHARLIE SOMETHING LESS FATAL LIKE
'SHOULD I HAVE A CRISP SANDWICH FOR LUNCH?'

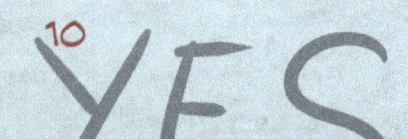

IT'S CALLED A DIVINATION GAME. THIS MEANS IT TELLS YOU YOUR FUTURE MUCH LIKE A OUIJA BOARD WOULD, OR THE OLD MAGIC 8 BALL TOY.

IF YOU'RE NOT SATISFIED WITH A YES OR NO ANSWER, YOU CAN TAILOR THE GAME TO SUIT YOU. FOR EXAMPLE, YOU MIGHT WANT TO QUIZ CHARLIE WHETHER YOU SHOULD ASK SOMEONE OUT ON A DATE.
YOU COULD PUT...
YES, NO,
YES, BUT WAIT UNTIL NEXT WEEK,
OR
NO, ASK HIS/HER BEST FRIEND OUT INSTEAD.

DID YOU KNOW, WATTERS, SOME THINK PLAYING CHARLIE CHARLIE IS CRAZY BECAUSE IT'S OPENING A PORTAL TO A DIMENSION OF DEMONS. YOU'RE INVITING THEM INTO THIS WORLD. THIS IS WHY YOU REALLY SHOULD 'END THE GAME' WHEN YOU HAVE FINISHED.
IT CLOSES THE DOORWAY. MAKE SURE YOU SAY 'IT'S TIME TO STOP, CHARLIE.' IT'S LIKE MAKING A PHONE CALL – YOU HAVE TO END IT!

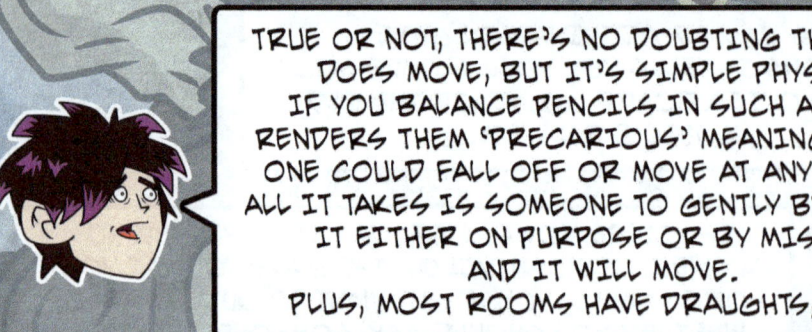

TRUE OR NOT, THERE'S NO DOUBTING THE PENCIL DOES MOVE, BUT IT'S SIMPLE PHYSICS! IF YOU BALANCE PENCILS IN SUCH A WAY IT RENDERS THEM 'PRECARIOUS' MEANING THE TOP ONE COULD FALL OFF OR MOVE AT ANY SECOND. ALL IT TAKES IS SOMEONE TO GENTLY BREATHE ON IT EITHER ON PURPOSE OR BY MISTAKE, AND IT WILL MOVE. PLUS, MOST ROOMS HAVE DRAUGHTS, RIGHT!

YUP! THEN THERE'S 'IDEOMOTOR REFLEX.' THIS IS YOUR BODY MOVING WITHOUT IT TELLING YOUR BRAIN! IT MIGHT BE A TINY MOVEMENT OF YOUR FINGER, BUT IT'S STILL A MOVEMENT.
THIS IS WHY A PLANCHETTE - THE BIT OF WOOD PEOPLE TOUCH WHEN MESSING AROUND WITH OUIJA BOARDS - MOVES.
IT'S NOT A GHOST! IT'S ONE OF THE HIGHLY EXCITABLE PEOPLE PLAYING THE DAFT GAME MOVING IT WITHOUT KNOWING!

AND WHY IS CHARLIE CHARLIE MEXICAN? HE'S GOT AN INCREDIBLY ENGLISH NAME. IF IT WERE MEXICAN SURELY HE'D BE CALLED CARLITO. OR JUAN ZEENUF BECAUSE ONE'S ENOUGH TO SCARE THE BREAKFAST OUT OF YOU! HA!

LOLLINGTONS ABOUND, MYCROFT.
SERIOUSLY THOUGH, CHARLIE CHARLIE BIT ME, OR WHATEVER IT IS, IS A LOAD OF OLD COBBLERS. IF THERE WERE AN ANCIENT DEMON TRYING TO GET TO YOU I'M SURE IT WOULDN'T NEED A COUPLE OF FLIPPING PENCILS TO DO IT.

SHEERLUCK SAYS:

THERE ARE MANY OTHER DIMENSIONS WITH A ZILLION ENTITIES DESPERATE TO MAKE CONTACT WITH OURS – DIMENSION PRIME – TO SAY HI OR TO TERRIFY US JUST FOR SPORT. OR STEAL OUR SOULS! I REFER TO AN ADVENTURE OF MINE TO EMPHASISE MY POINT.

CASE NAME : Let's Play True Or False!

MAIN ENTITY : Charlie Charlie

MAIN LOCATION : Bassleton School

SHEERLUCKIAN TOOLS USED : My Intellect

EVENTS :
WHEN YOU'RE NEW AT A SCHOOL YOU'RE QUIET TO BEGIN WITH, AREN'T YOU? NOT MOZZA.
THIS KID WAS LOUD, OVERLY CONFIDENT AND 100% UNLIKABLE FROM THE OFF. HE INTRODUCED HIMSELF BY HIS NICKNAME, WHICH WAS BAD ENOUGH, BUT WHEN I SAW THE ED SHEERAN* BADGE ON HIS BLAZER I KNEW I HATED HIM.

BY FIRST BREAK HE WAS INSISTING EVERYONE PLAY CHARLIE CHARLIE. SEVERAL OF THE KIDS WHO HAD CONDESCENDED TO DO SO SEEMED TO WALK AWAY NOW LOOKING DULL AND LIFELESS. AS THOUGH THEY'D LOST EVERY SPARK OF LIFE THEY HAD. LIKE PEOPLE WHO WORK IN LIDL. I WAS SUSPICIOUS AND WANTED TO KNOW MORE.

* IT'S ALWAYS TRICKY WHEN FRAGGLE ROCK ESCAPEE ED SHEERAN HAS A NEW ALBUM OUT ISN'T IT? SHOULD I NOT BUY IT ON CD, OR SHOULD I NOT DOWNLOAD IT? I USUALLY DON'T BUY IT AT A CAR BOOT SALE THE FOLLOWING SUNDAY.

HE TOLD ME TO ASK CHARLIE TO COME AND PLAY, SO I HUMOURED HIM.
THE TOP PENCIL MOVED TO YES AND WHAT HAPPENED NEXT SEEMED - FOR MOZZA AND ME - TO OCCUR IN REAL TIME OF ABOUT 15 MINUTES. I LATER FOUND OUT, TO THE ONLOOKERS SURROUNDING US, IT TOOK A SPLIT SECOND.
THE GAME WAS ON.

IN A FLASH OF TEMPORAL ENERGY MOZZA AND I WERE IN THE BETWIXT. THIS IS THE SPACE IN BETWEEN DIMENSIONS. IN THIS CASE THE BETWIXT SEPARATING THE PRIME DIMENSION AND DAVE THE DARK PLACE.
IT WAS LIKE THE SET OF A TV GAME SHOW. I KID YOU NOT. I WAS THE CONTESTANT, MOZZA WAS THE HOST AND ATOP A HUGE THRONE WAS CHARLIE CHARLIE HIMSELF. A MASSIVE, SLOBBERING, SOUL-HUNGRY DEMON.
I WAS TOLD THAT I HAD ENTERED INTO A BINDING AGREEMENT TO PARTICIPATE BY ASKING CHARLIE TO PLAY. THE STAKES WERE MY IMMORTAL SOUL OR IMMEDIATE FREEDOM.
I HAD TO GIVE A STATEMENT THAT CHARLIE JUDGED TO BE TRUE OR FALSE.
IF TRUE I COULD GO FREE. IF FALSE MY SOUL WOULD BE SLOWLY TRANSPOSED TO THE DARK PLACE ATOM BY ATOM. I WOULD LIVE OUT MY EXISTENCE A DULL, LISTLESS ZOMBIE UNTIL I PEGGED IT AND THE FINAL SPECK-OF-STARDUST WOULD BE CHARLIE'S.

THEY SHOWED ME SOME HIGHLIGHTS OF PREVIOUS UNLUCKY CONTESTANTS.
A BOY FROM MY TUTOR GROUP, LES KEEN, MADE THE STATEMENT 'I LIKE CHIPS WITH GARLIC SAUCE.'

CHARLIE RETORTED THAT WHILST LES DID LIKE CHIPS WITH GARLIC SAUCE, IF HE HAD TO EAT NOTHING ELSE FOR THE REST OF HIS LIFE HE'D SOON HATE THE DISH.
THEREFORE THE STATEMENT WAS JUDGED FALSE AND LES LOST THE GAME AND HIS SOUL.
A GIRL TWO YEARS ABOVE ME NAMED MARY-ANNE METCALFE SAID 'SHE'D BEEN TO HONG KONG.' CHARLIE SAID SHE'D BEEN TO THE TOURISTY HONG KONG, BUT NOT THE AUTHENTIC, TRADITIONAL HONG KONG YOU REALLY HAVE TO SEEK OUT.
MARY-ANNE LOST.

YUP, CHARLIE AND MOZZA HAD A NASTY, UNFAIR SCAM GOING HERE. BUT THEN THEY MET ME.

HERE'S A TRANSCRIPT OF WHAT HAPPENED.

MOZZA
MICHAEL CASSON-WATSON, OR 'SHEERLUCK', AS YOU'RE KNOWN, FOR WHATEVER REASON. LET'S HEAR YOUR STATEMENT.

SHEERLUCK
IN A MOMENT, MOZZA, OR 'DIPSTICK' AS YOU'RE KNOWN FOR QUITE APPARENT REASONS. CHARLIE, IMAGINE THE KUDOS YOU'D GET WITH THE OTHER SCARY MONSTERS IF YOU TOOK DOWN MY SISTER WATSON AND ME? WE STOP THINGS LIKE YOU DOING THINGS LIKE THIS. SO, I OFFER MINE AND WATSON'S SOULS.

CHARLIE
UPPING THE STAKES HEY? NICE. WHAT'S IN IT FOR YOU?

SHEERLUCK
IF I MAKE A STATEMENT THAT YOU CANNOT JUDGE TO BE EITHER TRUE OR FALSE, I WIN AND YOU END THIS UNFAIR CHARADE. YOU RELEASE EVERY LIVING SOUL YOU HAVE A CONTRACT ON AND YOU TAKE MOZZA TO DAVE THE DARK PLACE FOR ETERNITY.

MOZZA
NO, SORRY, WE ---

CHARLIE
SHUT UP, MOZZA, NO ONE LIKES YOU. OKAY, SHEERLUCK. IT'S A DEAL. LET'S HEAR YOUR STATEMENT THAT I CAN JUDGE NEITHER TRUE NOR FALSE.

SHEERLUCK
MY STATEMENT IS THIS… YOU WILL TAKE MY SOUL TO DAVE THE DARK PLACE.

THERE WAS A MOMENT'S PAUSE THEN MOZZA CACKLED ANNOYINGLY. HE DIDN'T GET IT.
CHARLIE'S SHOULDERS HUNCHED AND HE SIGHED.
HE GOT IT AND HE KNEW HE WAS BEATEN.

IF CHARLIE JUDGED
'YOU WILL TAKE MY SOUL TO DAVE THE DARK PLACE' TO BE TRUE, THEN HE WOULD HAVE TO LET ME GO. BUT BY LETTING ME GO HE'D BE MAKING THE STATEMENT FALSE BECAUSE I WOULD BE GOING HOME AND NOT TO THE DARK PLACE.

IF CHARLIE JUDGED
'YOU WILL TAKE MY SOUL TO DAVE THE DARK PLACE' TO BE FALSE, THEN HE WOULD TAKE MY SOUL TO THE DARK PLACE, BUT BY DOING SO HE WOULD BE MAKING THE STATEMENT TRUE. AND IF IT WAS TRUE, THEN I GET TO GO HOME.

CHARLIE CHARLIE COULD NOT WIN.
IN AN INSTANT THE GAME SHOW SET FOLDED IN ON ITSELF. CHARLIE'S GNARLED TALON WRAPPED AROUND THE BAFFLED MOZZA AND I WAS RETURNED TO THE SPLIT SECOND I STARTED PLAYING THE GAME. MOZZA WAS GONE.

LES, MARY-ANNE AND THE OTHER KIDS WERE BACK TO NORMAL AND I ASSUME COUNTLESS OTHER SOULS ALL OVER BRITAIN WERE TOO.
I MADE A DIRE ENEMY THAT DAY OF MOZZA, OR TO GIVE HIM HIS FULL NAME JAMES MORIARTY.

THE SHEERLUCKIAN ARMOURY

PSYCHOMETER

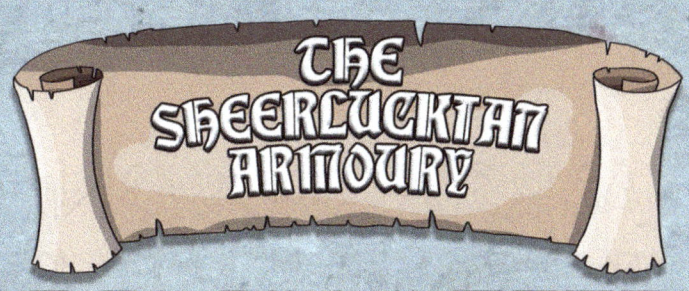

* POT NOODLE
* CHICKEN AND MUSHROOM
* STRANGE TEXTURE
* WATSON HAS IT

A WATCH THAT CAN TELL THE HISTORY OF AN OBJECT.
THE WEARER TOUCHES THE FACE OF THE WATCH ONTO SOMETHING, FOR EXAMPLE A DOOR, AND THE READOUT TELLS YOU EVERYTHING ABOUT ITS ENTIRE STORY.
SHEERLUCK ONCE USED IT TO UNCOVER IT WAS WATSON WHO ATE HIS POT NOODLE.
SHE DIDN'T NEED IT TO UNCOVER WHO PUT ALL HER MAKE-UP DOWN THE LOO.

WHO'S WHO
MRS HUDSON

SHEERLUCK, WATSON AND MYCROFT HAVE A GAPING HOLE IN THEIR MEMORIES. THEY'VE LIVED WITH THE RAT-EATING GHOUL MRS HUDSON ALL THEIR LIVES, BUT ACTUALLY KNOW VERY LITTLE ABOUT HER. SHE DOESN'T TALK. SHE JUST DOES HOUSEHOLD CHORES AND OCCASIONALLY HELPS OUT ON CASES.

THEY *DO* HAVE A VERY OLD PHOTOGRAPH OF A YOUNG FEMALE PARANORMAL INVESTIGATOR THAT VAGUELY RESEMBLES MRS HUDSON, BUT THEN...WHO KNOWS?

AND WHERE SHEERLUCK AND WATSON'S PARENTS ARE IS ANYONE'S GUESS.

THEY HAVE NO RECOLLECTION OF EVER HAVING ANY.

MAYBE ONE DAY THE TRUTH WILL BE LEARNED.

FARADAY BAGS

Used with Chief Spootue Tool, Faraday Bags are paranormal-pocket-satchels that can contain certain spooky baddies. For example, once a ghost is turned into a statue and smashed, the pieces are placed inside Faraday bag and will remain dormant until the team wish to restore the entity.
Larger and more solid monsters like ghouls, werewolves, demons etc are irresistibly drawn to the bags and sucked inside. No matter how big the beast, they are supernaturally-compressed and sent to sleep.
They are totally, 100% unharmed. Ish.

THE CLONE ZONE

THE MAD SCIENTIST ALSET ALOKIN HAS CLONED WATSON. ONLY 1 OF THEM IS THE REAL SIDEKICK SISTER, **THE OTHER 3 ARE ALMOST IDENTICAL COPIES.** FIND THE ODD ONE OUT SO SHEERLUCK CAN ZAP THE OTHERS WITH ALSET'S VERY OWN RAY GUN. HURRY, SHEERLUCK'S ABOUT TO BLAST THE LOT OF THEM SO HE CAN GET HOME IN TIME FOR TIPPING POINT.

PUZZLE PAGE

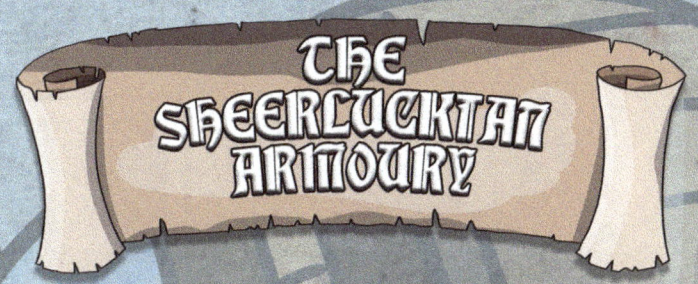

DIMENSIONAL DOOR KNOB

Liberated from Idaho Oakley's Traveling Cabinet of the Freakin' Strange, this artefact can be set to any known dimension with its intricate settings.

You then slam it into the Betwixt (the space between all dimensions) and it will open a doorway to your desired destination.

GEF THE TALKING MONGOOSE

MYCROFT'S mini Files

SPOOKINESS 05
REAL DANGER 00
A.D.P. LEVEL 04
HOKUM RATING 06

IN 1931, ON THE ISLE OF MANN, THE IRVING FAMILY CLAIMED TO HAVE A NEW, AND SOMEWHAT ODD, MEMBER.
IT WAS A DISEMBODIED VOICE COMING FROM THE WALLS.
AT FIRST THEY HEARD SCRATCHING AND THOUGHT IT WAS MICE, BUT WHEN THE CHATTING BEGAN THEY KNEW IT WAS SOMETHING OTHER WORLDLY.

THE VOICE TOLD THEM HE WAS A SPIRIT TRAPPED ON EARTH IN THE SHAPE OF A YELLOW MONGOOSE,
(A WILD MAMMAL SIMILAR TO MEERKATS, ABOUT THE SIZE OF A SMALL RAT.)

GEF THE TALKING MONGOOSE

HE CALLED HIMSELF GEF AND WOULD ONLY SPEAK, AND SHOW HIMSELF, TO THE FAMILY.
BUT, SEVERAL RESIDENTS SWORE THEY HAD SEEN HIM AROUND THE FARMHOUSE.
SEVERAL CLAIMED THEY'D EVEN HEARD HIM TALKING FROM THE WALLS.
GEF LOOKED AFTER THE FAMILY BY KEEPING RODENTS OUT AND ALERTING THEM WHEN PEOPLE WERE APPROACHING.
HE WOKE THE FAMILY IF THEY OVERSLEPT TOO.
IS YOUR FAMILY PET THAT USEFUL?

Sheerluck says

OH GEF.
YES, HE'S REAL.
WHEN THE FAMILY MOVED OUT IN 1945 GEF WENT TO LIVE IN THE NOT WHERE NOW HAS HIS OWN RADIO SHOW.

TELEPORT BY NUMBERS

ALSET ALOKIN – THE EVIL 'ELECK-TRICKERY' ARTIST – HAS ZAPPED OUR YOUNG HERO SHEERLUCK WITH HIS TELEPORT-BY-NUMBERS-TORCH.
THE VICTORIAN ROTTER DELIBERATELY HASN'T SET A DESTINATION CODE! SHEERLUCK WILL BE TAKEN APART BY NUMBERS AND WILL REAPPEAR IN A TOTALLY RANDOM LOCATION IN NO ORDER AT ALL! QUICK, JOIN THE DOTS TO STOP ALOKIN'S TERRIBLE *PLOT-TO-DOT!*

PUZZLE PAGE

BLACK EYED CHILDREN

SPOOKINESS 10
REAL DANGER 07
A.D.P. LEVEL 08
HOKUM RATING 02

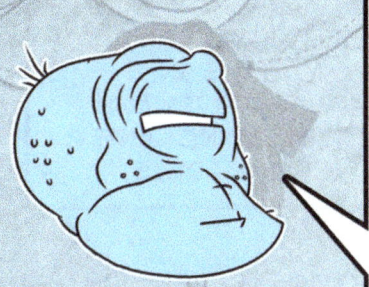

> PICTURE THIS.
> YOU'RE SITTING WATCHING TELLY AT HOME. IT'S LATE AT NIGHT. THERE'S A KNOCK ON THE DOOR.
> STANDING SILENTLY ON THE STEP ARE TWO YOUNG KIDS. A BOY AND A GIRL. ABOUT 8 YEARS OLD.
> JUST LOOKING AT YOU.
> WEIRD. WEIRDER STILL...THEIR EYES – THEY ARE COMPLETELY BLACK.

 I'M NOT SURPRISED.
KNOCK ON OUR DOOR AT THAT TIME OF NIGHT YOU'LL GET A BUSTED LIP TOO.
CHEEKY LITTLE RATS.

NO, NOT BRUISED BLACK EYES.
THERE'S NO WHITE AROUND THEIR PUPILS.
EACH PEEPER IS DARKER THAN A VAMPIRE'S UNDIES.
THERE'S NO SCLERA – THAT'S THE POSH NAME FOR THE WHITE OF AN EYE.
THE WHOLE EYE IS BLACK.

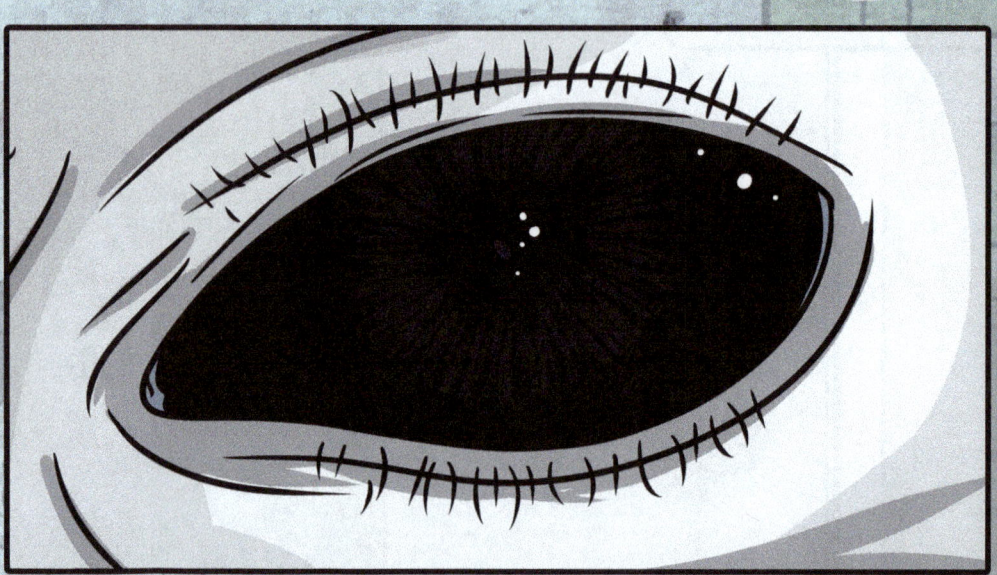

 SHUDDERSVILLE, MAN!
IT GETS CREEPIER TOO. IN LOW, MONOTONE VOICES THE LITTLE CREEPS ASK TO COME IN.
THEY REALLY WANT YOU TO SAY THAT THEY CAN – OUT LOUD. IT'S AS THOUGH THEY CANNOT ENTER YOUR HOME UNLESS YOU SAY YES. EERIE.

GIVES ME THE SHIVERS JUST THINKING ABOUT IT, WATTERS!
DID YOU KNOW, THERE'S AN OLD LEGEND THAT EVIL MAGICIANS AND VAMPS CANNOT ENTER YOUR HOME UNLESS YOU SPECIFICALLY SAY, 'YEAH, COME IN, WHAT'S THE WORST THAT COULD HAPPEN?'

IN VERMONT, AMERICA, A MARRIED COUPLE HEARD A HEAVY BANGING ON THEIR FRONT DOOR.
THEY WERE SHOCKED TO SEE A BOY AND A GIRL STOOD OUTSIDE.
CREEPILY, THEY ASKED TO COME INSIDE.

I HEARD ABOUT THIS! WHEN THE COUPLE ASKED WHERE THE KIDS' PARENTS WERE THEY COLDLY REPLIED, 'THEY WILL BE HERE SHORTLY.'

ONCE IN THE HOUSE THE CHILDREN ASKED TO GO TO THE TOILET. MEANWHILE THE HUSBAND'S NOSE STARTED BLEEDING.
HE FELT SICK AND DIZZY.
THE NORMALLY FRIENDLY FAMILY CATS WERE VISIBLY SCARED AND LEGGED IT. THEN, LIKE IN A HORROR FILM, THE HOUSE WAS PLUNGED INTO DARKNESS AS THE POWER FAILED.

THE WIFE FOUND THE KIDS STANDING MOTIONLESS IN THE HALLWAY. ONE SAID, 'OUR PARENTS ARE HERE NOW.' SHE LOOKED OUT THE WINDOW AND SAW TWO OMINOUS MEN IN BLACK TYPE BLOKES AT THE END OF THE DRIVE BY A BIG BLACK, OLD-FASHIONED, CAR. THE SINISTER KIDS GOT IN AND IT JUST DROVE OFF. BUT IT DIDN'T END THERE, DID IT WATSON?

 IT DID NOT, MYCROFT! AFTER A FEW DAYS THE HUSBAND'S NOSE BLEEDS GREW STEADILY WORSE. HE BECAME GRAVELY ILL.

THE DOCTOR WONDERED IF HE'D BEEN OVER USING SUNBEDS, OR WORKED WITH RADIATION. NEITHER OF WHICH WAS THE CASE. IT'S AS THOUGH THE KIDS HAD EMITTED SOME KIND OF DEADLY, INVISIBLE, RADIOACTIVE FIELD.

 THE WIFE BECAME ILL TOO, IN A WAY PEOPLE WHO HAVE ENCOUNTERED UFOS HAVE FALLEN SICK. IT'S CALLED MOON-BURN-SYNDROME. EVEN ONE OF THE CATS PEGGED IT. THIS MUST ONE OF THE ODDEST THINGS TO HAVE HAPPENED SINCE...WELL...EVER.

ALL BEC (BLACK-EYED CHILDREN) STORIES ARE DOWNRIGHT WEIRD. ONE TIME A LAD WAS SAT IN HIS MUM'S CAR WAITING FOR HER TO FINISH IN THE HAIRDRESSERS. A STRANGE LITTLE BOY WAS SUDDENLY AT THE WINDOW OF THE CAR.

 OMG! I KNOW THIS ONE. DIDN'T THE FREAKY LITTLE BEC ASK TO BE LET IN, BUT THE LAD WAS SO TERRIFIED HE HID ON THE FLOOR. WHEN HE DARED LOOK UP THE KID WAS GONE. HIS MUM RETURNED TO THE CAR LOOKING VERY FLUSTERED. SHE SAID A CHILD, WITH ODDLY DARK EYES, WALKED INTO THE HAIRDRESSERS AND DEMANDED THE KEYS TO HER CAR.

"THINK ABOUT IT! HOW DID THE BEC KNOW WHO OR WHERE THE MOTHER WAS UNLESS THERE'S SOME KIND OF TELEPATHIC MIND READING GOING ON? SHUDDERSVILLE TO THE POWER OF INFINITY!"

"THESE LITTLE WEIRDOS DEFINITELY BELONG IN 666 MONSTERS AVENUE, SPOOKY TOWN."

SHEERLUCK SAYS:

"OH THE BEC MYSTERY HEY? FORGOT TO SAY I SOLVED THIS ONE YONKS AGO. **I REFER TO AN ADVENTURE OF MINE TO EMPHASISE MY POINT.**"

CASE NAME : Bob a Job Week

MAIN ENTITY : Black Eyed Children

MAIN LOCATION : 221B Baker Street

SHEERLUCKIAN TOOLS USED : Gracie's Googlies/ Dimensional Door Knob

EVENTS :
I WAS AT HOME ENJOYING THE TRANQUILLITY OF AN EVENING'S SWEET SOLITUDE. WATSON, MYCROFT AND MRS HUDSON HAD TAKEN MR GEEZER TO INVESTIGATE THE HAUNTING OF ST. MARKS.
A BORING SOUNDING RUN-OF-THE-MILL HAUNTING UNWORTHY OF MY ATTENTION.
I DECIDED TO STAY IN AND ENJOY MY ROBERT THE MASTER CRAFTSMAN DVDS IN RARE, GLORIOUS PEACE.

NORMALLY YOU CAN HEAR VISITORS APPROACHING THE HOUSE, CRUNCHING UPON THE GRAVELLED DRIVEWAY.
THEN COMES THE DOORBELL.
TONIGHT... JUST CAME THE DOORBELL.
EERIE.
I OPENED THE DOOR TO A MOST CURIOUS PAIR OF YOUTHS, BOTH WITH EYES BLACKER THAN BARBECUED SAUSAGES.
A BOY AND A GIRL AGED 6 OR 7-ISH. BOTH WERE DRESSED IN OLD-FASHIONED CLOTHING THAT I SURMISED WAS FROM THE 1940S OR 50S. THEY HAD AN UNSETTLING, ALMOST, ROBOTIC WAY ABOUT THEM.

'LET US IN, FATTY-BUM-SHOVEL,' SAID THE BOY.
THE GIRL TURNED SLOWLY TO HIM AND SAID, 'DO NOT BE RUDE, JOHN LOUIS. BE POLITE. REMEMBER THE TALK WE HAD?'
THE BOY SAID, 'FORGIVE ME, FATTY-BUM-SHOVEL. WE WILL BE POLITE AND WILL NOT PUNCH YOUR PETS OR WEE ON THE CARPET.'
'PROMISE,' ADDED THE GIRL.

I PONDERED THE TWO FOR A MOMENT THEN REPLIED, 'IF YOU LIKE,' WITH A COOL SHRUG OF THE SHOULDERS.
THROUGHOUT THEIR VISIT THEY FIRED OFF AN ENDLESS BARRAGE OF RANDOM QUESTIONS WITHOUT EVER REQUIRING AN ANSWER.
IT WAS A THOUGH THEY COULD READ MY THOUGHTS, TAKING THE RESPONSES FROM THERE.
QUESTIONS LIKE :
DO YOU KNOW ANYONE IN PRISON?
WHAT'S THE SPICIEST FOOD IN THE WORLD?
DO YOU PREFER PENS OR PENCILS?
IF WE LIVED HERE WHICH ROOM WOULD WE HAVE?

They walked around and around the house exploring every nook and cranny. As my patience faded, and the desire to slap them grew, I stopped them in their tracks.

'What is it that you freaky-ga-ga-chumpers want?' I demanded.
They stood looking at me silently for a moment then the boy offered, 'Bob a job week.
Got any jobs you want doing for cash, fatty-bum-shovel?'
Then I really knew these kids were out of, not only place, but time.

Bob-a-job week started in the early 20th century and ended in the 1990s. Kids, mainly scouts and brownies, would knock on people's doors and ask to do odd jobs for a small amount of money.

A bob is an old fashioned name for a British 5 pence coin, or a shilling.
It started to dawn on me that these kids were a product of some bizarre genetic engineering experiment from way back. Again the 1940s or 50s sprang to mind.

MY HEART SANK FOR THESE POOR WRETCHES.
THEY WERE OBVIOUSLY KEPT IN A LIMBO STATE AND HOUSED IN A MILITARY ESTABLISHMENT SOMEWHERE WHERE THEY HAD BEEN FOR 60 OR 70 YEARS. NEVER AGEING AND WITH NO MEMORIES OF WHO THEY WERE. UNTHINKABLE.
I DECIDED TO PUT AN END TO THIS GROTESQUE INJUSTICE.
NOT BEFORE I GOT THEM TO DECORATE THE DOWNSTAIRS LOO FOR TEN BOB (50 PENCE.) AW COME ON, NEVER LOOK A GIFT HORSE IN THE GOB. OR EYE, LOL.

AFTERWARDS, I TREATED THEM TO ROBERT THE MASTER CRAFTSMAN ON DVD FOR A WHILE. THEY WERE ENTHRALLED. WE ATE BISCUITS APLENTY AND DRANK GALLONS OF TEA.
THEN, ALL OF A SUDDEN, THE GIRL STOOD UP AND SAID,
"OUR PARENTS ARE HERE, FATTY-BUM-SHOVEL."
SURE ENOUGH A LARGE BLACK, OLD-FASHIONED, CAR PULLED UP OUTSIDE AND TWO BURLY, MEN IN BLACK, (MIBS), GOT OUT.
THE CHILDREN SILENTLY AND OBEDIENTLY GOT INTO THE CAR, BUT WHEN I TRIED TO STOP THEM THE OMINOUS MIBS STOPPED ME.
I'M NOT MENACED EASILY AND GRACE'S GOOGLIE TOOK CARE OF THEM.

I PERSUADED A THIRD MIB, THE DRIVER, NOT TO MIX IT WITH ME AND HE DROVE US ALL TO A TOP-SECRET MILITARY INSTALLATION IN THE MIDDLE OF THE ENGLISH COUNTRYSIDE.

IT WAS CUNNINGLY DISGUISED AS A TOP-SECRET MILITARY INSTALLATION SO NO ONE WOULD ACTUALLY BELIEVE IT REALLY WAS TOP SECRET MILITARY INSTILLATION. FIENDISHLY CLEVER.

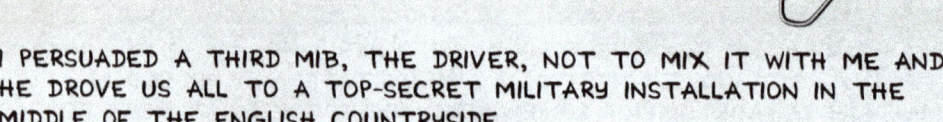

I DUCKED DOWN IN THE CAR AS HUGE ARMY SENTRIES WAVED US THROUGH.

AFTER A GOOD OLD MOOCH ABOUT I UNCOVERED THIS WAS A SECRET GOVERNMENT PARANORMAL ACTIVITY CENTRE CALLED THE DEPARTMENT OF URBAN CURIOSITIES.*

AFTER SEVERAL RUN-INS WITH MORE MIBS, MAD SCIENTISTS, FAILED EXPERIMENTS, HILARIOUS MUTATIONS AND A CRAZED SUPERVISOR CALLED DOCTOR CALIGARI, I LOCATED THE BLACK-EYED CHILDREN'S WARD.

I FOUND HUNDREDS OF THEM IN A LARGE UNDERGROUND BUNKER LYING IN OLD STYLE HOSPITAL BEDS.

THEY WERE CREATED AFTER WW2 TO CATCH ESCAPING NAZIS HIDING IN PSYCHIC BUBBLE DISGUISES. SINCE THAT TIME THEY'VE DONE VERY LITTLE APART FROM OCCASIONALLY WANDERING OUT OF THE BASE FOR BOB-A-JOB WEEK.

*MORE ABOUT THIS WEIRD ORGANISATION ANOTHER TIME.

- I MANAGED TO SPRING EVERY SINGLE ONE OF THEM INTO A POCKET DIMENSION CALLED THE OTHER SIDE. THERE, EVERY LIVING ENTITY IS OBSESSED WITH TV. THE CHILDREN ABSOLUTELY LOVE THE PLACE. THEY'RE BLISSFULLY HAPPY AND REGARDED AS CELEBRITIES BY THE OTHER SIDERS. THEY'RE THE STARS OF 'BLACK EYES', A REALITY TV SHOW ALL ABOUT THEM. BLESS.

- IT'S A HAPPY ENDING. NO LONGER ARE THEY TAKEN FOR GRANTED. I HAVE A FEW OF THEM OVER FOR A VISIT TO OUR DIMENSION FROM TIME TO TIME.

WHEN THE GARDEN NEEDS DOING.

MYCROFT'S mini Files

THE VIOGE, A FLESH EATING SCARECROW

SPOOKINESS 09
REAL DANGER 07
A.D.P. LEVEL 04
HOKUM RATING 06

THE CHANNEL ISLAND OF JERSEY IS HOME TO SOME OF THE MOST FASCINATING AND CREEPS-INDUCING LEGENDS EVER.
THERE'S THE SCREAMING HOUSE ON GHOST HILL FROM WHICH PITIFUL WAILING AND CRYING RANG OUT SO LOUDLY THAT LOCALS LOST SLEEP. THINGS GOT SO BAD THEY KNOCKED THE MOUTHY MANSION DOWN
- TWICE!

THEN THERE'S THE SNARLING SPECTRE OF A VICIOUS BLACK DOG THAT PROWLS ON THE HILLS OF BOULEY BAY. AS RECENT AS 2008 EYE-WITNESSES CLAIMED THE HELLHOUND CHASED THEIR CAR AS THEY DROVE BY! BAD DOG!
BY FAR THE MOST SINISTER IS THE FOLKTALE OF THE VIOGE, A TERRIBLE, FLESH-EATING SCARECROW.

MYCROFT'S mini Files

THE VIOGE, A FLESH EATING SCARECROW

THE VIOGE IS SUPPOSED TO LIVE IN A HIDDEN LAIR ALONG A STEEPLY INCLINED PATH CALLED CRACK ANKLE LANE.
ANYONE FOOLHARDY TO WALK THE PATH IS RISKING THEIR LIVES AND ENDING UP AS TOMORROW'S MURDEROUS SCARECROW POO!
THE VIOGE IS ALLEGED TO LOOK LIKE A SPINDLY, LANKY, TRADITIONAL SCARECROW WITH A DEMON'S FACE.
SHUDDERSVILLE, MAN!

Sheerluck says

MY ADVICE TO ANYONE INTENDING TO WALK ALONG CRACK ANKLE LANE IS:
ONLY GO WITH SOMEONE YOU CAN OUTRUN.

WHO'S WHO

FOW-ST

KIND HEARTED AND FUNNY STEPHEN FOWLER WAS A STRUGGLING STAGE MAGICIAN WHEN HE WAS VISITED BY A DEMON.
IT OFFERED HIM GRAVITY AND TIME-DEFYING MAGICAL POWERS IN RETURN FOR HIS SOUL WHEN HE PEGS IT.
NOT MAJOR POWERS, JUST ENOUGH TO BECOME A RATHER ENTERTAINING STREET MAGICIAN. FOOLISHLY HE ACCEPTED. CHANGING HIS NAME TO FOWLER-STREET-MAGICIAN, THEN JUST FOW-ST, HE BEGAN PERFORMING IN PUBLIC.
HOWEVER, THE TRICKSTER DEMON ALSO GAVE HIM AN AWFUL, SNIDE AND VICIOUS PERSONALITY AND THE PUBLIC HATED HIM!
NOW FOW-ST IS A MASTER CRIMINAL DESPERATE TO FUND HIS WORK IN TRACKING DOWN THE DEMON WHO CONNED HIM.

Where's Where → Coliseum of the Damned

A chunk of dark-matter seemingly adrift in pan-dimensional space/time.

It is not.

It is orbiting every world and times period waiting for the chance to snatch folk and creatures and turn them into performing gladiators.

It's presided over by the crazed Emperor Necro, protected by his army of monster legionnaires.

About the size of two blocks of flats, this terrifying arena will just appear where Necro wants it to.

Your street for example.

They come for you while you're asleep and convince you that you are dead. To get to Heaven you must succeed in the Great Games.

These can be sword fights, jousting and bobbing for apples – in acid!

You could be there a very long time, but if you win your freedom they will return you to moment they took you in your sleep and it will all seem like a nightmare – the memory of which quickly fades.

That's how they keep getting away with it.

Sheerluck has vowed to one day shut down the Coliseum of the Damned.

Where's Where → COLISEUM OF THE DAMNED

MYTHAMATICS

SHEERLUCK IS ENJOYING A SHORT BREAK AT THE MYTHICAL CREATURE HOLIDAY RESORT CENTAUR PARKS. BUT, HE'S FORGOTTEN HIS PASS-CODE NUMBER FOR HIS ROOM.

EACH OF THESE MYTHICAL CREATURES HAS A MYTHAMATIC VALUE. BY AN AMAZING FLUKE OF PROBABILITY THEIR COMBINED NUMBER IS ALSO THE NUMBER OF SHEERLUCK'S ROOM.

IT'S EASY! JUST ADD UP THEIR NUMBERS TO GET THE 3 DIGIT CODE THE BOY DETECTIVE NEEDS TO GET INTO HIS ROOM! WRITE IT ON THE KEYPAD! HURRY, THE BOY DETECTIVE IS BUSTING FOR A WIDDLE!

THE LIE-NOCULARS

OH NO, NOT ANOTHER PESKY, EXHIBIT FROM IDAHO OAKLEY'S TRAVELLING CABINET OF THE FREAKIN' STRANGE!

THESE ARE LIE-NOCULARS AND THEY NEVER SHOW YOU THE COMPLETE TRUTH.

ONE LENS IS ALWAYS DIFFERENT TO THE OTHER - JUST TO CAUSE CONFUSION.

THE LAST TIME THIS PAIR WAS USED GENERAL INCOMPETENCE LED HIS ARMY INTO A RAGING VOLCANO.

HE WENT WITH THE LENS SHOWING A STURDY, FLAME-PROOF BRIDGE ACROSS IT.

OF COURSE - THERE WAS NO BRIDGE AND ALL 300 MEN WENT INTO THE MOLTEN LAVA ONE AFTER THE OTHER.

PUZZLE PAGE

THIS IS COUNT MEOWT'S SPOOKY CASTLE.
CAN YOU SPOT THE 5 SUBTLE DIFFERENCES BETWEEN THE LENSES?

Where's Where → THE NOT

THE NOT IS AN UNSTABLE DIMENSION POSSIBLY ON THE BRINK OF TOTAL IMPLOSION.
THIS MEANS IT WOULD COLLAPSE IN ON ITSELF RENDERING EVERYTHING AND EVERY CREATURE IN IT PULVERISED TO NOTHINGNESS.
SO, NOT A GREAT PLACE TO LIVE.
TWO ABSTRACT PLANES MAKE UP THE NOT.
THE SOLID NOT AND THE WHAT NOT.

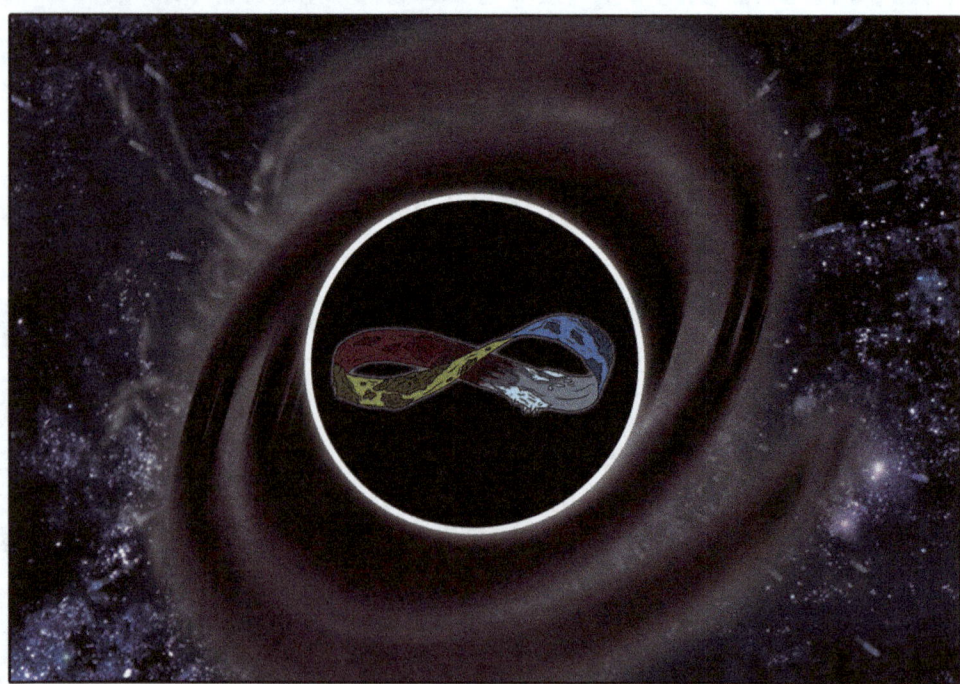

THE SOLID IS A MOBIUS LOOP THAT'S HOME TO CONTINENTS, TOWNS, KINGDOMS, SWAMPS AND MURKY, MONSTER-INFESTED OCEANS.
TECHNOLOGY-WISE IT'S AT DIFFERENT STAGES OF HUMAN HISTORY ALL LIVING SIDE BY SIDE.
ONE TOWN MIGHT BE MEDIEVAL OR VICTORIAN, THE NEXT ONE COULD BE MODERN OR EVEN STONE-AGE.
HUMANOID CREATURES LIVE THERE, BUT THEY ARE NOT HUMAN AND INVARIABLY NOT TO BE TRUSTED.
THE WHAT NOT IS THE SOUP-LIKE SPACE AROUND THE LOOP WHERE NOTHING EXISTS
- EXCEPT MYCROFT - FLOATING LIKE A BABY IN A BATH.

Where's Where → NOTLAND YARD

Many centuries ago, to combat the rising criminal element in the Not, a law enforcement agency was established, Notland Yard.

They normally keep Not villains where they should be. Occasionally, criminal creatures and evil entities escape to our world so Notland Yard sent an inspector to enlist Sheerluck's help.

The three we know best are Inspector Lestrade, Inspector Gregson and the sinister and bad-tempered Inspector Corls.

| INSPECTOR CORLS | INSPECTOR LESTRADE | INSPECTOR GREGSON |

OR A SNOWFLAKE, SOCIAL JUSTICE WARRIOR, CORPORATE HATING, GLUTEN-FREE, VEGAN, VEGETARIAN, SECRETLY MUNCHING ON A MACCY-D, BUT NOT WANTING HER RIGHT-ON COMRADES TO KNOW ABOUT IT.

COULD BE, MYCROFT.
THANKS FOR RUINING THE CREEPY ATMOS, BY THE WAY.
IN THIS CASE IT'S A GHOUL. A VICIOUS, STENCH RIDDEN, MONSTER THAT LIVES UNDERGROUND.
IT LIES IN WAIT FOR NEW BODIES TO BE BURIED BEFORE TUNNELLING TOWARDS THEM WHEN THE MOURNERS HAVE GONE.
THEN IT WILL FEAST ON THE DECOMPOSING MEAT AND BONES.

CRIKEY, WATSON, DON'T EVER GET A JOB WRITING GREETING CARDS.
YES, GHOULS ARE DISGUSTINGLY STOMACH CHURNING.
DID YOU KNOW, SOME GHOUL MYTHOLOGIES SAYS GHOULS CAN SHAPE-SHIFT INTO ANIMALS LIKE WOLVES.
A BIT LIKE VAMPIRES.

I KNOW, BUT VAMPS ATTACK THE LIVING.
GHOULS ONLY EAT DEAD PEOPLE.
MIND YOU, THEY SAY THAT IF A PERSON SURVIVES A GHOUL BITE HE THEN BECOMES ONE.
THAT'S VERY MUCH LIKE VAMPIRES, WEREWOLVES AND ZOMBIES.
IT'S LIKE A PASSING ON A TERRIBLE DISEASE.
SHUDDERSVILLE, MAN!

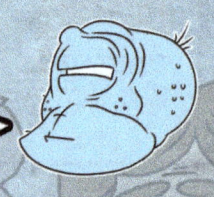

SOME SAY THE GHOUL CAN ACTUALLY TAKE ON THE FACIAL FEATURES OF SOMEONE IT HAS JUST DEVOURED.
THAT'D BE A GREAT PRANK WOULDN'T IT – STORMING INTO THE FUNERAL WAKE OF SOMEONE THEY'VE JUST BURIED AND SHOUTING, 'WHAT THE HECK DID YOU DO THAT FOR? I WAS ONLY HAVING A LIE-IN!'

LOLLINGTONS, MYCROFT! DID YOU KNOW THE ACTUAL NAME 'GHOUL' COMES FROM ARABIC, MEANING JINN OR DEMON.
THEY ARE THOUGHT TO BE THE CHILDREN OF IBLIS, THE ISLAMIC VERSION OF THE DEVIL.
INDEED, MANY CULTURES HAVE LEGENDS OF TERRIBLE MUNCHING MONSTERS THAT LURK AROUND CEMETERIES AT NIGHT DEVOURING THE DEAD.
SOME RELIGIONS CLAIM GHOULS ARE BAD PEOPLE WHO WERE NOT ALLOWED INTO HEAVEN. THEY WERE CAST BACK DOWN TO EARTH IN HORRIFIC FORMS AND ONLY ALLOWED ROTTING FLESH FOR DIN-DINS.

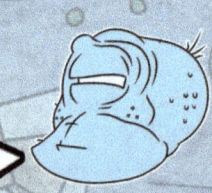

THROUGHOUT HISTORY FOLK HAVE BEEN TRIFFIED BY WHAT HAPPENED TO THEIR BODIES AFTER PEGGING IT.
THE GHOUL LEGEND WAS MADE VERY REAL IN VICTORIAN TIMES WHEN BODY SNATCHING WAS A POPULAR TRADE.
MEDICAL SCIENCE WASN'T PROGRESSING AS FAST AS MEDICAL STUDENTS WOULD HAVE LIKED BECAUSE THERE WASN'T ENOUGH STIFFS TO PRACTICE ON.

 OH YES, THE BODY SNATCHERS. STUDENTS WOULD PAY MEN TO ROB GRAVES AND DELIVER THE CORPSES TO THEIR LABORATORIES. THEN THEY COULD OPEN THEM UP AND SEE HOW EVERYTHING WORKS.
PEOPLE WERE VERY SUPERSTITIOUS IN THOSE DAYS AND THOUGHT THAT UNLESS YOU WERE LAID TO REST IN PEACE, IN ONE PIECE, YOUR SPIRIT WOULD NEVER GET TO HEAVEN.

NOWADAYS MOST PEOPLE WOULDN'T CARE IF YOU FLUSHED THEM DOWN THE LOO, BUT BACK THEN IT WAS A BIG DEAL.
PEOPLE WANTED TO BE BURIED SEVERAL FEET DEEPER THAN NORMAL, OR EVEN UNDER CONCRETE. IRON RAILINGS WERE PLACED OVER SOME GRAVES TO DETER THE EVIL RESURRECTION MEN.

 THANKFULLY LAWS AND IDEALS CHANGE. WE BECAME MORE ENLIGHTENED AND PEOPLE BEGAN TO DONATE THEIR BODIES – AFTER THEY'D PEGGED IT OF COURSE – TO MEDICAL SCIENCE. THIS MEANT BODY-SNATCHING BECAME A DYING TRADE.
HA!

 YOU HAVE A GHOULISH SENSE OF HUMOUR SOMETIMES, WATTERS.
LOLLINGTONS.
INDEED, ANYONE WHO HAS A MORBID INTEREST IN ANYTHING TO DO WITH GRAVEYARDS OR PEGGING IT IS OFTEN CALLED A GHOUL.
GOTHS AND EMOS FOR EXAMPLE.
I THINK THAT'S UNFAIR BECAUSE DEATH IS PART OF LIFE.
YOU CAN'T AVOID IT SO WHY NOT HAVE A LAUGH ABOUT IT.

 PRECISELY! GO GOTHS! HOORAY FOR EMOS!
AND, WE KNOW FROM PERSONAL EXPERIENCE THAT GHOULS ARE REAL.
THERE'S WHOLE COMMUNITIES OF THEM IN DAVE THE DARK PLACE AND THE NOT.
HECK, OUR HOUSEKEEPER MRS HUDSON IS A GHOUL.

 YES, BUT LET US POINT OUT SHE DOES NOT ROB GRAVES.
ONCE WE CAN FIND OUT WHY SHE'S IN SUCH A GHOULISH STATE WE CAN CURE HER SO UNTIL THAT TIME SHE IS ON A STRICT DIET OF DEAD RATS.

 SHE DID GET THAT CAR THIEF ONCE. REMEMBER THAT?

 YES! THANK YOU, WATSON. IN HER DEFENCE HE WAS A VERY BAD PERSON. IT WAS A ONE OFF.

 THEN SHE GOT THAT KIDNAPPER. THEN THOSE ARMED ROBBERS, ALL SEVEN OF THEM. HA!, MRS HUDSON'S GNAWED HER WAY THROUGH A GOOD FEW DEAD VILLAINS IN HER TIME.

 IT'S NOT FUNNY, WATSON. IT'S IN VERY BAD TASTE.

 NAH, BY THE LOOK ON HER FACE EACH TIME THEY TASTED VERY GOOD!

SHEERLUCK SAYS:

 YES GHOULS ARE VERY REAL AND A BIG PROBLEM. I REFER TO AN ADVENTURE OF MINE TO EMPHASISE MY POINT.

CASE NAME : New Ghoul In School

MAIN ENTITY : Ghouls

MAIN LOCATION : The Not

SHEERLUCKIAN TOOLS USED : Bian Lian Deerstalker / Mrs Hudson

EVENTS :
PICTURE THIS. TV COOKERY JUDGE GREG CHARLATAN DIES. GREG, WHO COULDN'T COOK, WAS FAMOUS FOR DISSING DISHES WHILST GREEDILY EATING THEM.
HIS CATCHPHRASE 'I'M JUST GLAD I'M NOT PAYING FOR THIS RUBBISH' BECAME A TV LEGEND.

GREG CHOKED ON A TOY FROM A HAPPY MEAL HE'D DEMANDED FOR FREE IN MACCY-D'S.
HE'D MISTAKEN THE SPIDERMAN FIGURE FOR A SIDE DISH.
AT HIS FUNERAL, THE COUNTLESS Z-LIST CELEBS PRETENDING TO HAVE MET, AND EVEN LIKED, HIM BECAME SPOOKED BY THE NOISES COMING FROM HIS COFFIN.
IT WAS OPENED AND OUT POPPED A GHOUL SHOWERING THE MORTIFIED ONLOOKERS WITH GREG'S GNAWED BONES.
IT SLOBBERED, 'I'M JUST GLAD I'M NOT PAYING FOR THIS RUBBISH' BEFORE DARTING OUT OF THE CHURCH AND DISAPPEARING INTO THE DARKEST RECESSES OF
THE GRAVEYARD.

HUNDREDS OF STORIES LIKE THIS BEGAN CROPPING UP AT FUNERALS ALL OVER THE GLOBE.
BY FAR THE WORST WAS THE KING OF TAURED'S STATE FUNERAL WHERE THE GHOUL, AFTER DEVOURING WHAT WAS LEFT OF THE KING, SCARED THE QUEEN TO DEATH AND PROMPTLY TUCKED INTO DESSERT.

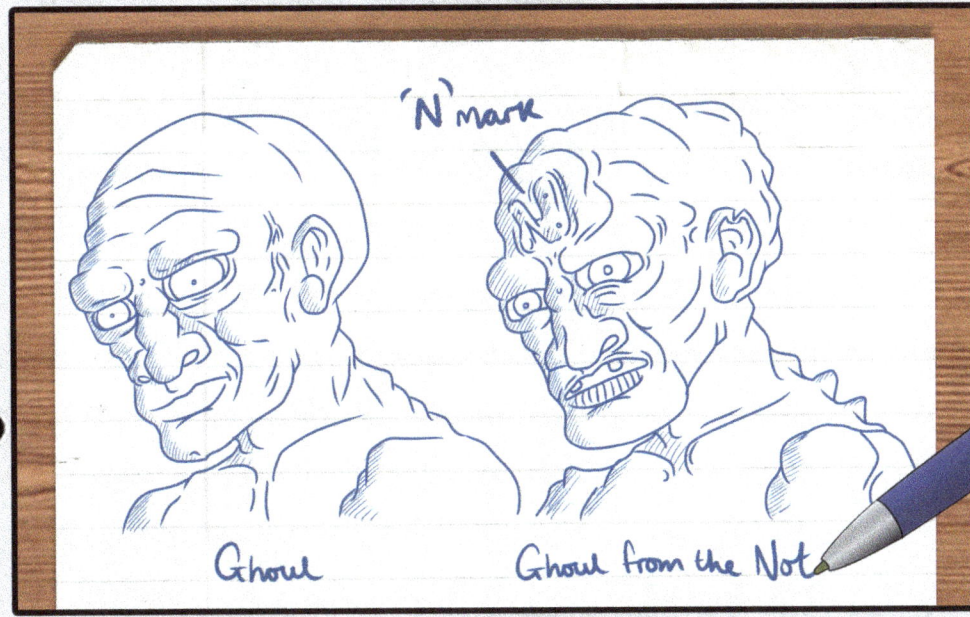

Ghoul — Ghoul from the Not — 'N' mark

IN EACH CASE THE GHOULS WERE IDENTIFIED AS HAILING FROM THE NOT.
THE N ON THEIR FOREHEADS BEING A DEAD GIVEAWAY. INSPECTORS LESTRADE, GREGSON AND CORLS OF NOTLAND YARD WANTED TO KNOW WHY HOMEGROWN GHOULS WERE BEHAVING LIKE THIS? HOW WERE THEY GETTING FROM ONE DIMENSION TO ANOTHER WITH PIN-POINT ACCURACY?
IN THE NOT, THEY'VE SET UP A GHOUL SCHOOL TO TEACH THEM TO BE DECENT CITIZENS.
NOTLAND YARD WANTED MRS HUDSON AND ME TO GO UNDERCOVER IN THE GRIMLY FIENDISH REFORM SCHOOL FOR GHOULS AND SEE IF I COULD FIND A LINK TO THESE ATTACKS.

USING MY BIAN LIAN DEERSTALKER I ASSUMED THE FAÇADE OF A GHOUL, ALBEIT A VERY HANDSOME ONE, AND BEGAN WORK.

MRS HUDSON WAS GIVEN A JOB AS A DINNER LADY SERVING ALTERNATIVE ROTTEN-MEAT-FREE BRANDS LIKE FAKEFLESH, NOTROT AND COUNTERFEET.

A GIRL GHOUL NAMED CHEW DATGUT BEFRIENDED ME. SHE WAS A SHY AND NERVOUS CHARACTER EAGER TO REFORM HER GHOULISH WAYS.
CHEW CONFIDED IN ME THAT SHE THOUGHT SOMETHING ODD WAS GOING ON WITH THREE GHOULS IN PARTICULAR.

PROFESSOR CADAVER: SENIOR COFFIN BOFFIN. POLITE ETIQUETTE TEACHER.

NORA BONE: THE STUDENT UNION LEADER AND GHOULISH SOCIAL JUSTICE WARRIOR. YUP, THERE'S EVEN SNOWFLAKES IN THE NOT.

MISS DIAGNOSE: SCHOOL NURSE. IF YOU'RE NOT ILL SHE HAS A CURE FOR THAT!

AFTER SHADOWING ALL THREE FOR A DAY OR TWO, WE CAME TO THE CONCLUSION THAT PROFESSOR CADAVER WAS DEFINITELY UP TO SOMETHING IN HIS CLASSROOMS LATE AT NIGHT. HE WAS OUR SLIME-SUSPECT. (YOU HAVE TO USE A LOT OF HORROR PUNS WITH GHOULS, IT'S HOW THEY TALK.)

SURE ENOUGH, WE ENTERED HIS ROOMS AND SAW A MOST INTRIGUING SIGHT! AN ARABIAN DAISY PUSHER.
ALSO KNOWN AS A BURKE & HARE GATE, THIS IS A SWIRLING HOLE PUNCHED THROUGH THE BETWIXT, THE MEMBRANE THAT SEPARATES DIMENSIONS. THEY ONLY WORK FOR GHOULS AS THEY ARE TUNED TO THE HARMONICS OF MORIBUNDIAN ATOMS. THEY'RE ALSO HIGHLY UNSTABLE, BUT CAPABLE OF GETTING A GHOUL TO ANY GRAVE OR COFFIN IN ANY UNIVERSE WITH PIN-POINT ACCURACY. DAISY PUSHERS ARE BANNED IN EVERY KNOWN DIMENSION BECAUSE OF THE ECOLOGICAL DAMAGE THEY HAVE ON THE BETWIXT. GHOULS ALSO GAVE UP USING THEM CENTURIES AGO BECAUSE THE CHANCES OF THEM FAILING WERE PHENOMENAL. ANYTHING INSIDE A COLLAPSED ONE WAS INSTANTLY ATOMISED OUT OF EXISTENCE.

AND WHICH ONE OF THE SUSPECTS WAS INSIDE THE PORTAL, SPINNING AROUND LIKE A SOCK IN A WASHING MACHINE?
ALL THREE OF THEM. AND WHO JOINED THEM A SECOND LATER WHEN A MUSHY FOOT HIT HIM IN THE BACK?
YUP. ME.
YOU SEE THE VILLAIN OF THIS CASE WAS...CHEW.
CHEW HAD BEEN SEVERAL STEPS AHEAD OF ME ALL THE WAY. SHE WAS NO REFORMING FLESH-MUNCHER!
QUITE THE OPPOSITE! SHE WAS A FANATIC WHO WANTED GHOULS FROM EVERY REALM TO RISE UP AND TAKE CONTROL. THOSE GRAVESIDE ATTACKS WERE HER FORM OF GHOULISH TERRORISM.

WITH ME OUT OF THE WAY THERE'D BE PRECIOUS FEW TO STOP A FULL UN-DEAD UPRISING!
ALL SHE HAD TO DO WAS CLOSE THE DAISY PUSHER.
THANKFULLY THOUGH, SOMETHING WAS WRONG! IT WASN'T RESPONDING. WHY WAS THAT?
IF THERE'S A GHOUL IN A DAISY PUSHER IT WILL RESPOND. OR COLLAPSE. THEN I TWIGGED IT.

THERE WERE NO GHOULS IN THERE.
PROFESSOR CADAVER, NORA BONE AND MISS DIAGNOSE WEREN'T REAL GHOULS! THEY WERE INSPECTORS LESTRADE, GREGSON AND CORLS. EACH OF THEM HAD INDEPENDENTLY SNUCK INTO THE SCHOOL, WEARING SIMILAR DISGUISES TO MY OWN, TO GRAB THE GLORY WHEN I FINALLY CRACKED THE CASE. CURSE THOSE VAIN IDIOTS.

BEFORE CHEW COULD FIGURE OUT A WAY TO DO US IN, SHE TOO FELT A GHOULISH HEEL IN HER BACK.
MRS HUDSON HAD CREPT IN AND HOOFED CHEW FORWARD INTO THE DAISY PUSHER.

INSTANTLY, WE FOUR WERE BLASTED OUT AS CHEW'S UN-DEAD ATOMS TRIGGERED THE PORTAL INTO ACTION. OR RATHER INACTION. IT COLLAPSED. THE DAISY PUSHER SLAMMED SHUT AND SHE WAS NO MORE.
THE GHOUL SCHOOL HEADMASTER, MR TOMBSCOFF, ORDERED A SCHOOL ASSEMBLY AS HE WANTED TO OFFER ME HIS HAND IN RECOGNITION OF MY WORK.
I'VE STILL GOT IT IN A JAR SOMEWHERE.

THE FATAL ADDER DAGGERS

THE FATAL ADDER DAGGERS ARE ATTEMPTING TO ESCAPE FROM IDAHO OAKLEY'S TRAVELLING CABINET OF THE FREAKIN' STRANGE! THEY'RE FURIOUSLY HEAD-BUTTING THE MAGIC GLASS AND IT'S NEARLY BROKEN!

FINISH THE ADDITION SUMS ON THE SEALING SCROLLS AND WRITE THE CORRECT ANSWERS IN THE DIGIT SPACES ATOP THE DISPLAY CASE. THIS WILL RESTORE THE GLASS AND KEEP THEM SAFELY IMPRISONED.

WATSON IS A MATHS WHIZZ AND COULD EASILY DO IT, BUT SHE'S HALF HYPNOTISED BY THE TERRIBLE WEAPONS! HURRY!

THE SHEERLUCKIAN ARMOURY

THE I-SCREAM-VAN

AS SHEERLUCK AND WATSON ARE KIDS, AND MYCROFT IS A TINY ATOMIC SPRITE, THEY DON'T HAVE DRIVING LICENSES. THEY NEEDED A VEHICLE TO GET AROUND IN AND SOMEONE TO DRIVE IT. IN KEEPING WITH THE UNUSUALNESS OF THEIR WORLD THEY CHANCED UPON THE I-SCREAM-VAN DRIVEN BY A HAUNTED ICE CREAM MAN CALLED MR GEEZER.
YUP, YOU COULDN'T MAKE IT UP, COULD YOU?
THEY FOUND IT INSIDE IDAHO OAKLEY'S TRAVELLING CABINET OF THE FREAKIN' STRANGE USING IT FOR A DARING ESCAPE. TO OPERATE MR GEEZER THEY TAKE HIS TUB OUT OF THE FREEZER, PLACE IT ON THE DRIVING SEAT AND HE OOZES UPWARDS INTO A HUMAN-ISH FORM.
THEY TELL HIM WHERE TO DRIVE AND HE OBEYS.
HE DOESN'T SAY MUCH, EXCEPT IF THEY ARE EVER PULLED OVER BY THE POLICE. THEN HE'LL JUST FREAK THEM OUT WITH RANDOM, WEIRD STUFF UNTIL THEY GO.

THE I-SCREAM-VAN

MR GEEZER HAS TO BE PREVENTED FROM SELLING ICED DELIGHTS TO KIDS AS WHEN THEY REALISE HE'S A HAUNTED ICE CREAM THEY ARE OFTEN TRAUMATISED FOR LIFE. THAT SAID, IF YOU WERE TO BUY ONE OF EVERYTHING ON THE MENU, HOW MUCH WOULD HAVE LEFT OVER FROM 1 ENGLISH POUND.
(THERE'S 100 PENCE IN 1 POUND IF YOU'RE OUTSIDE OF BRITAIN.)

WHO'S WHO
THE YORKSHIRE DRAGOON

The ghost of the brave 18th century private soldier, Sir Tom Brown.

At the battle of Dettingen, Germany, in 1743, Brown single-handedly retrieved the Union flag from the French. It cost him his nose, an ear, some fingers and damn nearly his life. He was shot at and stabbed by the enemy, but Brown did it, he got back the flag for the British!

Brown was knighted on the field and given an ample pension and a silver nose as a reward. Sheerluck first met him when his ghost was ransacking shops and businesses trying to get royal wedding union flags. Turns out some useless councillor had had Brown's picture removed from the town hall because it 'glorified war.' Only a buffoon disses the Dragoon.

THE GREEN CHILDREN OF WOOLPIT

SPOOKINESS 07
REAL DANGER 00
A.D.P. LEVEL 03
HOKUM RATING 08

SUFFOLK, ENGLAND, THE 12TH CENTURY.

LABOURERS WORKING IN THE FIELDS FOUND A YOUNG BOY AND GIRL WANDERING AIMLESSLY.
THE KIDS WERE CONFUSED, SPOKE A LANGUAGE NO ONE HAD EVER HEARD BEFORE, AND THEY WERE GREEN.
YUP, AS GREEN AS THE HULK'S BUM! THEY WORE ODD CLOTHES MADE FROM MATERIALS THE VILLAGERS HADN'T SEEN BEFORE.

A KIND KNIGHT NAMED RICHARD DE CAINE GAVE THEM A HOME. AT FIRST THEY'D ONLY EAT RAW BEANS, BUT EVENTUALLY STARTED EATING MEAT AND BREAD.

The Green Children of Woolpit

Soon their green skin faded and turned pink.
Sadly, the boy didn't take to our world and pegged it.
The girl grew up and learned English.
She said they were from an underground world called St Martin's Land where it is always dark and everyone is green.
They got lost and ended up in a tunnel, emerging from it in our world.
The girl eventually married but alas, there's no more info on the story.
Where they extra-terrestrials, fairy folk or from another dimension?

Sheerluck says

Probably just lying vegetables from Dave the Dark Place.
Most of the veg there is into some sort of scam.
I once lost my watch to a potato.
Yeah, just a pair of hustle sprouts.

AINT THAT TRUE, MYCROFT. MANY RELIGIONS AND BELIEF SYSTEMS SAY IT'S THE SOUL THAT LEAVES THE BODY.
OTHERS SAY IT'S SOMETHING CALLED THE SUBTLE BODY WHICH IS YOUR MIND.
WHATEVER YOU MIGHT BELIEVE, IT'S A FORM OF YOUR CONSCIOUSNESS THAT LIFTS OUT OF YOUR SLEEPING PHYSICAL BODY AND GOES FLOAT-ABOUT.

EVER HAVE A DREAM THAT YOU WERE FLYING AROUND THE HOUSE OR THE STREETS OR SOME WEIRD PLACE? PERHAPS IT WASN'T A DREAM – PERHAPS THAT WAS ACTUALLY YOU ASTRAL PROJECTING.

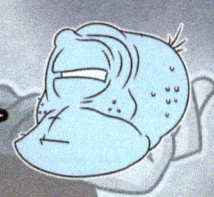

COULD BE! THERE'S A BIG DIFFERENCE BETWEEN ASTRAL PROJECTING AND JUST DREAMING, RIGHT MYCROFT?

ABSOLUTELY. DREAMING IS STAYING INSIDE YOUR OWN HEAD. YOU NEVER LEAVE YOUR BODY. YOU REMAIN IN YOUR SUBCONSCIOUS, YOUR MIND CONSTRUCTS THE PLACES, THE PEOPLE, THE CREATURES AND THE FEELINGS YOU EXPERIENCE.

 EXACTLY! IT'S ALL MADE OUT OF EVERYTHING YOU'VE EVER SEEN OR HEARD ALL MIXED UP. THAT'S WHY, IN DREAMS, YOU MEET THINGS LIKE A THREE WHEELED SHARK WITH A CLOWN'S HEAD SINGING A MEDLEY OF DAVID BOWIE SONGS WHILST FLINGING FISH FINGERS AT YOU.

 I'VE MET THAT CLOWN SHARK AND HE'S GOT A GREAT VOICE.
AN ASTRAL PROJECTION IS NOT OF YOUR MAKING. IT'S A TRIP TO A PLACE CALLED THE ASTRAL PLANE.
HERE IT ALL GETS A BIT FUZZY.

 IT DOES A BIT.
YOU SEE, SOME SAY THERE ARE DIFFERENT LEVELS OF THE ASTRAL PLANE, 7 IN FACT, EACH ONE MORE WONDERFUL THAN THE LAST.
YOU ONLY GET TO REACH 7TH HEAVEN IF YOU'RE A REALLY COOL AND LOVELY HUMAN.
SO IF YOU'RE A BADDY WHO SMOKES AND BEATS PEOPLE UP YOU'LL ONLY GET TO LEVEL ONE.
BE NICE AND YOU'RE GOING TO THE TOP! YAY!

THE PLANES ARE SUPPOSEDLY INHABITED BY ANGELS, OTHER SOULS AND LOADS OF OTHER MAGICAL ENTITIES.
YOU GET TO REMEMBER ALL YOUR PAST LIVES TOO, APPARENTLY.
WHY DON'T YOU REMEMBER THEM RIGHT HERE, RIGHT NOW ON EARTH?
BECAUSE YOUR CURRENT BRAIN IS PART OF THIS CURRENT EXISTENCE AND IT DOESN'T HAVE ACCESS TO THAT INFO.
THINK OF ASTRAL PROJECTING AS SUDDENLY GETTING ACCESS TO A FANTASTIC COMPUTER WITH LOADS OF NEW PROGRAMS AND SOFTWARE, AND ACE WI-FI TOO.

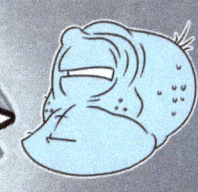

YOU HUMANS ARE ALL ANCIENT SOULS THAT ARE CONSTANTLY REPACKAGED ON EARTH TO LIVE LIFE AFTER LIFE AFTER LIFE.
WHEN YOU PEG IT YOU WILL SEE EVERYTHING FOR WHAT IT IS.
YOU'LL REALISE WHAT IT'S ALL ABOUT.
THAT'S THE THEORY ANYWAY.

I HEARD THAT TOO.
YOU GET THE CHANCE TO HAVE YOUR SOUL SENT BACK TO EARTH TO HAVE ANOTHER GO AND BE A BETTER PERSON.
OR, YOU CAN ZOOM OFF AND EXPLORE ALL THE ASTRAL PLANES YOU'VE BEEN AWARDED ACCESS TO.

WELL, WHAT DO YOU THINK?
WOULD YOU LIKE TO ASTRAL PROJECT AND GET AN AMAZINGLY ENLIGHTENING GLIMPSE INTO THE VASTNESS OF THE OMNIVERSE?

OR DO YOU WANT TO INVISIBLY SPY ON SOMEONE?
YOU COULD SEE IF YOUR MATES ARE TALKING ABOUT YOU.
OR GET INTO THE PICTURES FOR NOTHING AND WATCH ALL THE NEW FLICKS FOR NOTHING.

SHEERLUCK SAYS:

"HMMM, I FEARED ASTRAL PROJECTION WOULD COME BACK AND BITE ME ON THE BUTTOCKS ONE DAY.
OH WELL, THIS STORY PROVES I'M HUMAN. IT'D BE BORING IF I WON EVERY TIME.
I REFER TO AN ADVENTURE OF MINE TO EMPHASISE MY POINT."

CASE NAME : The Ghost That Wasn't Dead

MAIN ENTITY : Irene Adler

MAIN LOCATION : The Rings Of Saturn Jewellery Shop

SHEERLUCKIAN TOOLS USED : Chief Spootue/I-Scream-Van

EVENTS :
DESPITE INCANTATIONS BEING IN PLACE TO KEEP THE PARANORMAL OUT OF OUR HOUSE, ENTITIES AND SPIRITS OCCASIONALLY DO GET IN.
I WAS VISITED BY THE TROUBLED GHOST OF A TEENAGE GIRL. TO SAY SHE WAS 'WELL FIT' WOULD BE AN UNDERSTATEMENT. SHE COULD HAVE GOT A JOB SELLING PERFUME IN BOOTS.

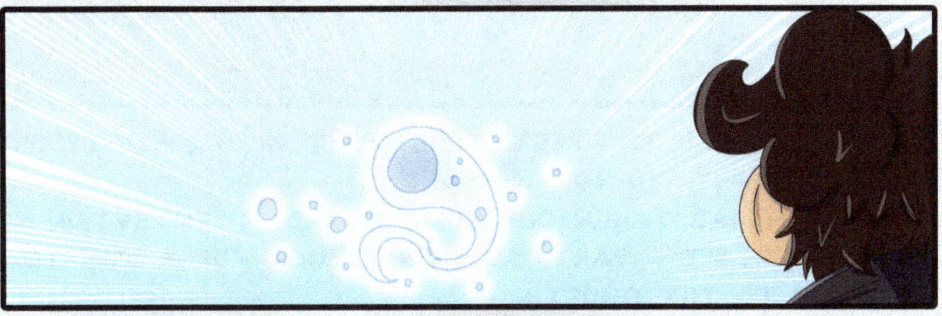

AT FIRST SHE APPEARED AS JUST A MERE, SMOKY WISP SO IT TOOK A WHILE BEFORE I EVEN KNEW SHE WAS THERE. SHE'D TRIED THE USUAL GHOSTLY METHODS OF GETTING ATTENTION. ROCKING AN EMPTY ROCKING CHAIR AND PULLING A TERRIFYING FACE IN THE BATHROOM CABINET MIRROR AS I SHUT IT. BUT, NAH, DIDN'T SEE HER. COULDN'T HEAR HER EITHER SO SHE WAS TOTALLY INCOMMUNICADO - UNABLE TO COMMUNICATE.

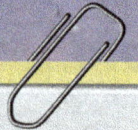

EVENTUALLY, USING ALL HER CONCENTRATION, SHE FORMED A PARTIAL APPARITION IN FRONT OF ME.
WELL, IN FRONT OF THE TELLY, WHICH I FOUND REALLY IRRITATING.
WHEN I SAW HOW GORGEOUS SHE WAS I LOST ALL HOSTILITY AND DECIDED TO TAKE THE CASE.

I ATTEMPTED TO FREEZE THE SPIRIT WITH CHIEF SPOOTUE. CURIOUSLY IT DID NOT WORK.
WATSON HAD TAKEN OUR OUIJA BOARD TO ENTERTAIN SOME TODDLERS AT A PARTY SO I WAS STUCK FOR A WAY TO SPEAK TO THE GHOST.
EVENTUALLY I MANAGED TO MAKE CONTACT WITH HER VIA A TIN OF ALPHABETTI-SPAGHETTI.
TALK ABOUT CREEPY PASTA.

I THEN KNEW WHY THE CHIEF HAD FAILED.
THIS GHOST WAS NOT A GHOST. IRENE ADLER,
THAT WAS HER NAME, WAS ASTRAL PROJECTING.
SHE SAID SHE'D RETUNED TO HER BODY TO FIND IT
HAD GONE. SHE SUFFERED TERRIBLY FROM SOMNAMBULISM,
WHICH MEANS SLEEPWALKING. WHILE SHE WAS OUT ON A
PROJECTION, HER BODY HAD WANDERED OFF SOMEWHERE
AND WITH NO MEANS OF WAKING UP.
IT HAD JUST KEPT GOING.

SHE INFORMED ME IT HAD GONE TO WHERE SHE WORKS,
A JEWELLER'S SHOP AND HAD BECOME LOCKED IN.
HER SOUL WAS PREVENTED FROM RE-ENTERING HER BODY
BY THE HI-TECH LASER SECURITY TRIPWIRES.
THEY WERE MESSING UP THE TRANSCENDENTAL
FREQUENCY NEEDED TO ACHIEVE ASTRAL PROJECTION.
SHE WAS AFRAID HER SOUL MIGHT BE CUT FREE BY THE
LASERS AND SET ADRIFT FOREVER.

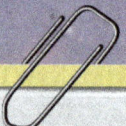

THIS SEEMED ODD TO ME.
I HAD NEVER HEARD OF THAT BEFORE. BUT, THIS BEGUILING, ANGELIC, WELL - TIDY BEAUTY CLAIMED IT WAS TRUE SO WHO WAS I TO DISAGREE. TIME WAS OF THE ESSENCE TOO AS AN ASTRAL DEMON NAMED RABIDBUMBARK HAD FOLLOWED HER BACK TO THIS PLANE AND WAS HEADED FOR HER EMPTY BODY.

THIS I KNEW WAS A REAL DANGER FOR PROJECTIONISTS. SOMETIMES DARK ANGELS AND MALEVOLENT ENTITIES GET TO A BODY BEFORE THE HUMAN SOUL CAN AND TAKE THEM OVER. THIS LEAVES THE PROJECTIONIST HOMELESS.
WE NEEDED TO DISABLE THE SHOP'S ENTIRE SECURITY SYSTEM AND FAST.
WE GOT INTO THE I-SCREAM-VAN AND SET MR GEEZER TO DRIVE US TO THE RINGS OF SATURN JEWELLERS SOME 20 ODD MILES AWAY.
THE JOURNEY WAS FRAUGHT WITH DANGER AS THE EVIL DREAM DEMON RABIDBUMBARK FLEW AT THE VAN CLAWING RIPS IN THE METAL AND SHATTERING THE GLASS TRYING TO MAKE US CRASH.
AN EXPERTLY TOSSED GRACE'S GOOGLIE TOOK CARE OF HIM.

ONCE WE WERE AT THE JEWELLER'S I MELTED MR GEEZER AND POURED HIM THROUGH THE LETTER BOX.

- AS HE COOLED DOWN HE REFORMED INTO HIS HUMANOID SHAPE AND CLUMSILY TURNED OFF THE SECURITY LASERS.

- I RUSHED IN AND SEARCHED FRANTICALLY FOR IRENE'S SLEEPING BODY. IT WAS NOT THERE. AND WHERE HAD HER GHOST GONE? I SOON GOT MY ANSWER WHEN THE BUSINESS END OF THE SHOP'S SWEEPING BRUSH CAME DOWN UPON THE BACK OF MY HEAD AND OUT WENT THE LIGHTS.

- WHEN I CAME ROUND THE PLACE WAS GUTTED OF ANYTHING REMOTELY SPARKLY. I'D BEEN DUPED. ADLER'S BODY WAS NEVER IN THE SHOP. SHE'D LEFT IT BEHIND THE WHEELIE BINS AROUND THE BACK. ONCE THE SECURITY WAS DOWN SHE GOT BACK INTO HER BODY, COSHED ME AND ROBBED THE SHOP. BLEARY EYED AND WITH A THUMPING HEADACHE I CALLED HER SOME EXTREMELY UN-P.C. NAMES AS SHE TOOK HER LEAVE.

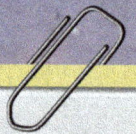

SHE STOPPED, KNELT DOWN BESIDE ME AND GAVE ME A PECK ON THE CHEEK. MISS ADLER SMILED AND SAID, 'GOODNIGHT SHEERLUCK.' SHE THEN PUNCHED ME IN THE FACE AND ONCE AGAIN EVERYTHING WENT BLACK.
I AWOKE ON THE FLOOR OF THE I-SCREAM-VAN.
WE WERE NEARLY HOME. MR GEEZER HAD PICKED ME UP AND DRIVEN AWAY FROM THE SCENE AT SPEED, THANK GOODNESS.
I LATER FOUND OUT THAT RABIDBUMBARK WAS A MYSTICALLY MODIFIED IMPOSEAL, HER PET.
SHE MUST USE THE WRETCHED THING IN HER CRIMINAL SHENANIGANS A LOT AS IT PLAYED ITS PART BEAUTIFULLY.

THERE WERE SO MANY WARNING SIGNS ABOUT ADLER'S STORY THAT I IGNORED. MY KEEN DETECTIVE REASONING FAILED ME BECAUSE I WAS BEGUILED BY A PRETTY FACE.
I VOW THAT IT SHALL NEVER HAPPEN AGAIN.
UNLESS SHE FANCIES A MACCY-D SOMETIME.
SHE'LL BE PAYING OF COURSE BECAUSE SHE'S BLOOMIN' LOADED NOW.

CHRISTMAS MOURNING

THREE FESTIVELY FESTERING GHOULS HAVE SNUCK OVER FROM THE NOT DIMENSION FOR THEIR CHRISTMAS DINNER. THEY'VE FOUND THE PERFECT PRESENT UNDER THE TREE IN THE CHURCHYARD.
THEY'RE TUNNELLING THEIR WAY TO THEIR YUKKY YULETIDE BANQUET RIGHT NOW,
BUT WHICH ONE WILL REACH IT FIRST?

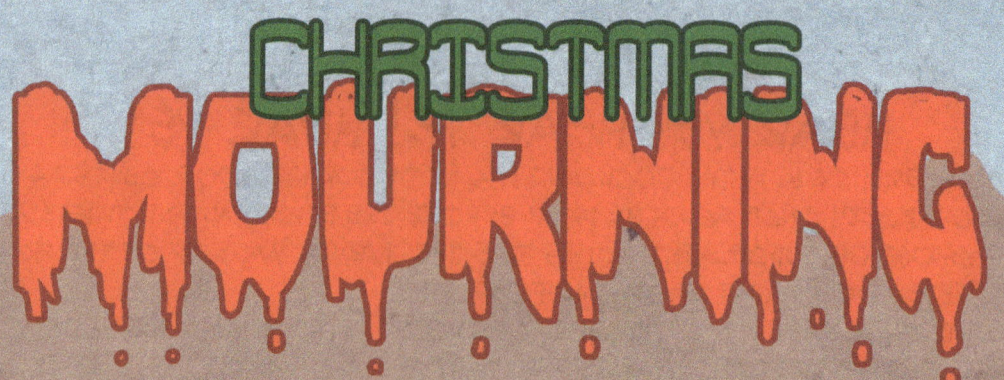

| RANCID VICIOUS | MZ AIRYGUTS | DJ REBEL N-TOMB |

FOOTNOTE : SICK? THINK OF IT AS GETTING A TAKE-AWAY PIZZA. YOUR MEAT-FEAST COMES IN A BOX TOO, DOESN'T IT?

WHO'S WHO

WITCH IZZIT

IZZIT HAILS FROM DAVE THE DARK PLACE AND BY JINGO WE WISH SHE'D STAY THERE.
SHE'S A CRUEL CONJURER OF CONUNDRUMS AND A MERCHANT OF MISERY. USING HER MAGIC SHE PRESENTS HUMANS WITH WEIRD AND SEEMINGLY IMPOSSIBLE PUZZLES.
SHE FEEDS OFF THEIR CONFUSED DESPAIR AND CONVERTS IT INTO HER OWN MAGICAL ENERGY.
SHE CAN'T BE REASONED OR BARGAINED WITH AND IS EVIDENTLY NOT RIGHT IN THE BRAIN BOX.

IMPOSEALS

PARANORMAL IMPS THAT DO NOTHING BUT SILENTLY LIE AROUND PULLING SILLY FACES AT YOU AND BEING TRIPPING HAZARDS.
WATSON HAS A PET IMPOSEAL CALLED BAD-LAD-JOHNNY-HOTDOGS.
A FEW TIMES A WEEK TAKE-AWAY FOOD ARRIVES FOR JOHNNY AND, CURIOUSLY, IT'S ALWAYS PAID FOR.
DON'T ASK US.

which is it?

WITCH IZZIT, SPITEFUL AS EVER, HAS FILLED WATSON'S ROOM WITH IMPOSEALS.
TO GET THEM TO VANISH BACK TO DAVE THE DARK PLACE SHE MUST IDENTIFY BAD-LAD-JOHNNY-HOTDOGS.
CAN YOU SPOT HIM?

PUZZLE PAGE

YOUR VINYL BREATH RECORD SHOP

SHEERLUCK IS IN THE STRANGE DIMENSION DAVE THE DARK PLACE. HE'S VISITING HIS FAVOURITE AND LEAST FAVOURITE RECORD SHOP, YOUR VINYL BREATH.
HE LOVES IT BECAUSE THEY STOCK EVERYTHING GOTH EVER RECORDED. HE HATES IT BECAUSE THE OWNERS ARE TWO GOTHULS (GHOULS INTO GOTH) WHO THINK THEY ARE FUNNY. THEY ARE ANYTHING BUT FUNNY!
THE BOY PARANORMAL INVESTIGATOR MUST FIND THE NAMES OF 10 OF HIS FAVE BANDS BEFORE THEY'LL SELL HIM ANY VINYL. SEE IF YOU CAN DO IT FOR HIM. HURRY, HIS PATIENCE IS WEARING THIN AND THERE'S TWO GOTHULS ABOUT TO GET A KNUCKLE SARNIE EACH.

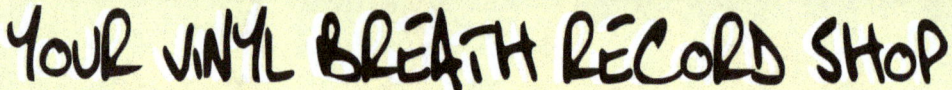

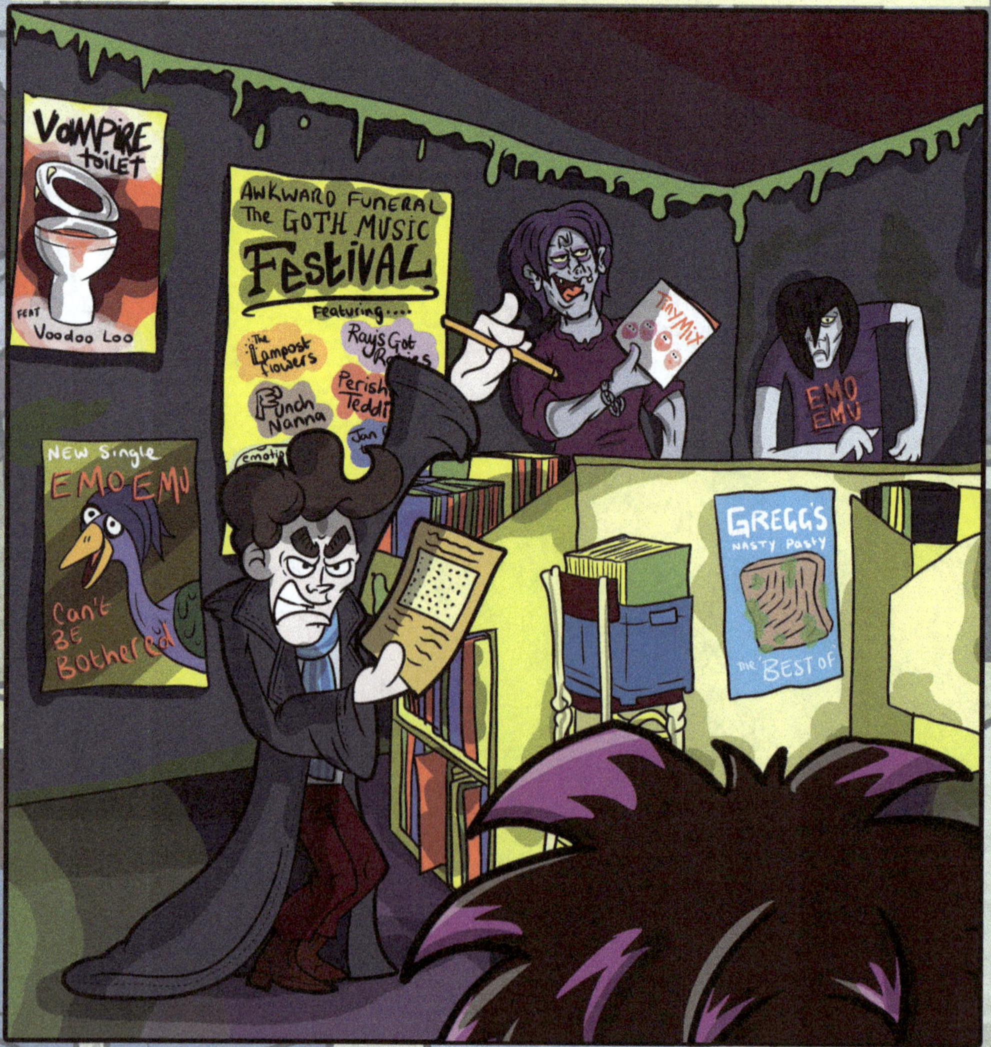

FIND THE GOTH BAND NAMES FOR SHEERLUCK

```
M K F G C I G A Q O M J Q Z X G F X T N
G L A M G R A V E H Y O M G G O A E C A
S J X W E Y A J P Z B B Z Y Y N U A J I
P A W D L M F J X U L M I B L K Z B M G
M R T Y U R G L B W O Y A S Z J I R C N
F O B A N S A Y B N O L K R A B B Q E I
D C R Q N T E A V F D A S T Y E I L U N
J V G I T F K T O H Y W J W A H F V Q E
W D N H B S R X A J T D P N S E V A I K
P F G B K U J O F M R M S R X L O Y E C
X K Y N O U N Y G H O A G W J L D O X I
X C I J Q J P D G A U N O L R S B N O S
Q T O E E E T G B T S E A S P E N M Z W
S X C X Y L E Z O I E H Z L C U P I K K
D L Z J Q H Z P D H R N P D L D U X F N
I G M D I A S H N Y S T B M F E K M A I
A X K O T Y X F B Q G H N W Y B I Q U
K X X W Y U I W I R O T J D S J U X O U
T E F F U B L L I K D A O R A Z J F U Z
M X Z Z D C X A U Z A O R D T Y F O H U
```

MORIBUND BIRTHDAY - **HELLSPUD**
MR BEAN'S AUTOPSY — **STINKSKAB**
BELLA NO-MATES - **ROADKILL BUFFET**
MY BLOODY TROUSERS - **GLAMGRAVE**
SICKENING IAN — **SATAN FROG**

HAVE YOU LIVED BEFORE?

Have you ever been somewhere for the first time and had an eerie feeling you'd been there before? Do you get odd memories out of the blue about doing strange things you're 100% sure you've never done.
Like eating raw turnips or dancing round a maypole.
Maybe breaking wind on a dinosaur for a dare then running away with your hairy neanderthal mates shouting 'UG D'MAN! UG D'MAN!'
If so then it's quite possible you've lived before.
Perhaps you soul has been reincarnated many times?
You could have had several lives in several time zones.
Take our **Neurological Unconscious Thought & Transcendental Extrasensory Remembrance Test.**
Yes, it is rather a long-winded name isn't, so we settle for the acronym the N.U.T.T.E.R. test.

Answer the questions honestly and see how you did at the end.

Warning : If you have vague memories of having a little moustache, a uniform, shouting a lot in German and invading places – don't take the test!
Some things are best left a mystery.

1) WHAT CLOTHES MAKE YOU FEEL THE MOST COMFORTABLE?

A) JIMMY-JAMMAS, WHICH IS PROBABLY HOW KING ARTHUR DRESSED MOST OF THE TIME.

B) A WOODEN BOX, NAILED SHUT WITH ME INSIDE. BLISS.

C) COMFY CASUAL CHAIN MAIL ARMOUR, ARMED WITH AXES AND SWORDS.

2) WHAT KIND OF DREAMS DO YOU USUALLY HAVE?

A) BEING LOCKED IN A LOO, PERHAPS BECAUSE OF RELIGIOUS PERSECUTION, OR SOMETHING.

B) I DREAM OF LYING STILL AND DOING NOTHING.

C) FLYING AN AEROPLANE, KAMIKAZE STYLE, INTO A BATTLESHIP AND SHOUTING, 'I'LL GET A PAY RISE FOR THIS!'

3) DO YOU HAVE ANY NATURAL TALENTS THAT MAY HAVE BEEN LEARNED IN A PREVIOUS INCARNATION?

A) I CAN FIT A FULL DIGESTIVE BISCUIT IN MY MOUTH WITHOUT BREAKING IT, LIKE CAVEMEN COULD. PROBABLY.

B) I CAN LIE VERY STILL FOR DAYS AND DAYS.

C) I RECKON I COULD RIDE A HORSE INTO A VILLAGE, BURN IT TO THE GROUND AND KILL EVERYONE. EASY.

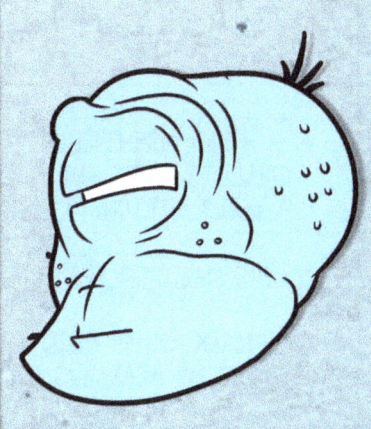

4) HAVE YOU EVER BEEN SOMEWHERE AND KNOWN IT LIKE THE BACK OF YOUR HAND?

A) MY MATE'S HOUSE NEXT DOOR. MAYBE I OWNED IT IN ANOTHER LIFE DESPITE ME BEING TWO YEARS OLDER THAN THE ENTIRE ESTATE.

B) THE GRAVEYARD.

C) YES, WHEN I WENT TO WHITECHAPEL, LONDON. I KNEW EVERY DARK ALLEY AND COULD ALMOST HEAR VICTORIAN POLICE WHISTLES AND CRIES OF 'JACK THE RIPPER HAS STRUCK AGAIN!'

5) DO YOU HAVE A STRANGE FEAR OR PHOBIA THAT YOU CAN'T EXPLAIN?

A) THE THEATRE! IT'S JUST SO FLAMING BORING, WHICH SUGGESTS I WAS PRESIDENT LINCOLN WHO GOT SHOT IN ONE.

B) A FEAR OF MOVING ABOUT WHEN I SHOULD BE LYING VERY STILL AND DECOMPOSING.

C) I HAVE A PHOBIA ABOUT BEING CHASED BY PEASANTS HOLDING BURNING TORCHES AND SCREAMING, 'GET THE FRANKENSTEIN MONSTER. GET HIM!'

6) DO YOU HAVE ANY UNUSUAL SCARS OR BIRTHMARKS THAT COULD BE FROM ANOTHER LIFE?

A) A WEIRD INDENTATION IN MY STOMACH THAT COLLECTS FLUFF AND IS EITHER A JOUSTING SCAR OR A BELLY BUTTON.

B) THE SMELL OF DEATH.

C) A MARK ON MY NECK THAT MIGHT HAVE BEEN WHERE MY HEAD WAS TAKEN OFF IN A GORY BATTLE AND AS IT FLEW THREW THE AIR IT SHOUTED, 'I'LL BE BACK!' IT ALSO MAY BE A RASH.

NOW CHECK YOUR ANSWERS:

MAINLY As

NO, SORRY, YOU'RE NOT REINCARNATION FODDER. WE CAN SEE YOU'D REALLY LOVE TO HAVE LIVED BEFORE, BUT THERE'S NO EVIDENCE OF IT HERE. AND DON'T GO RUSHING TOWARDS GETTING ANOTHER LIFE - ENJOY THE ONE YOU'VE GOT NOW. HECK, YOU ONLY GET ONE. WELL, YOU DO ANYWAY.

MAINLY Bs

ERM, WE DON'T HOW TO BREAK THIS GENTLY TO YOU, BUT WE THINK YOU MIGHT BE DEAD. YOU JUST LIE THERE STINKING OF ROT AND IT'S NOT A GOOD SIGN. ON THE PLUS SIDE YOU COULD BE ABOUT TO BE REBORN AGAIN. YAY! THAT'LL BE A LAUGH. WON'T IT?

MAINLY Cs

OH YEAH, YOU'RE A PROLIFIC REINCARNATEY TYPE AND NO MISTAKE. TROUBLE IS YOU'RE A LOONY TOO. YOU DON'T ALWAYS HAVE TO BE A VIOLENT SOCIOPATH YOU KNOW! NEXT TIME ROUND COME BACK AS A USED KIPPER SALESMAN OR A NICE LADY WHO DESIGNS WOOLLY HATS OR SOMETHING. BE YOU'LL BE MUCH HAPPIER AND THE DEATH TOLL WILL DROP RIGHT DOWN.

HOW DID YOU DO?

PUZZLE ANSWERS

THE CLONE ZONE - THIRD FROM THE LEFT.

TELEPORT BY NUMBERS

NOTLAND YARD IDENTITY PARADE - THE LEFT REYNARD

MYTHAMATICS - SHEERLUCK'S ROOM CODE IS **154**

THE LIE-NOCULARS

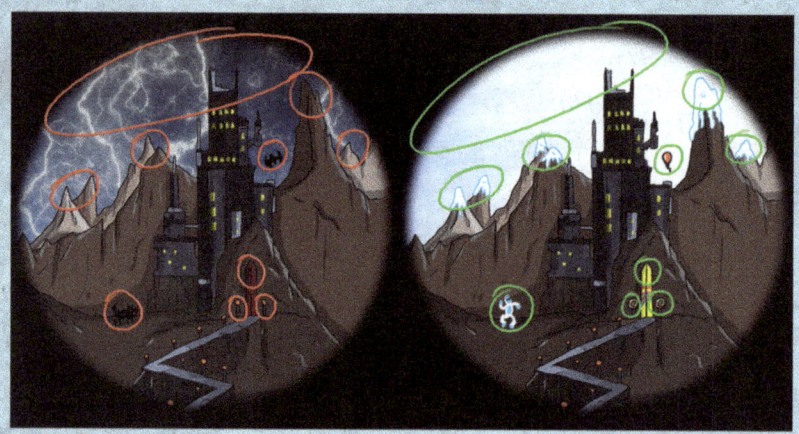

THE FATAL ADDER DAGGERS - 9   71   257

THE I-SCREAM-VAN - 15+6+5+4+2+8+10+20=70

70-100=30

UNION FLAG FIND

JUDGE MENTAL

CHRISTMAS MOURNING - ROUTE A

WHICH IS IT?

FIND THE GOTH BAND NAMES.

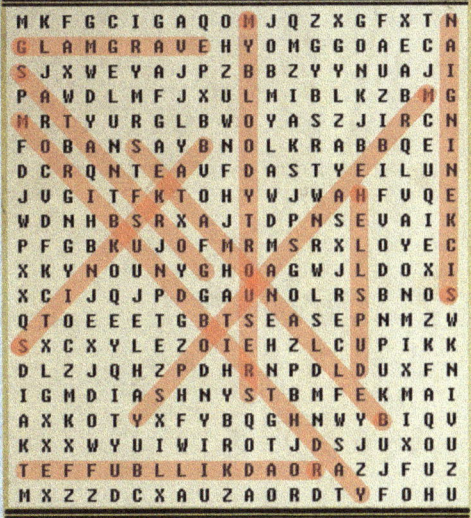

OTHER GREAT BOOKS FROM THE AUTHOR

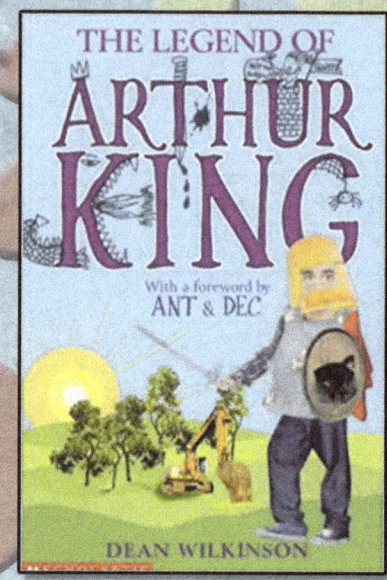

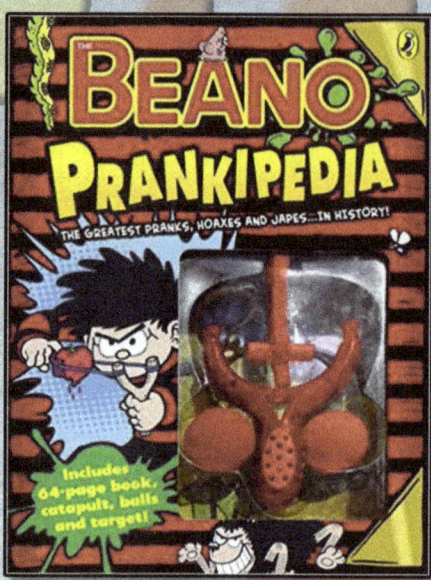

THE LEGEND OF ARTHUR KING

ARTHUR KING AND THE CURIOUS CASE OF THE TIME TRAIN

THE BEANO : PRANKIPEDIA

PLANTS VERSUS ZOMBIES : BOOK OF THINGS...QUIZ BOOK

THE CLASSIC CHILDREN'S TELEVISION QUIZ BOOK

VISIT **DEANWILKINSON.NET** FOR MORE ONFO.

THE SHEERLUCK BOOKS ARE AVAILABLE IN ALL
GOOD BOOK SHOPS IN THIS DIMENSION,
THE NOT AND DAVE THE DARK PLACE.
ALTERNATIVELY JUST GO ON AMAZON.

SEE
WWW.SHERLOCKHOLMESBOOKS.COM
&
WWWW.SHEERLUCKPI.COM

FOR DETAILS OF FUTURE SHEERLUCK BOOKS,
GRAPHIC NOVELS AND ALL MANNER OF
PARANORMAL PARAPHERNALIA.

www.ingramcontent.com/pod-product-compliance
Lightning Source LLC
LaVergne TN
LVHW061346060426
835512LV00012B/2581